CONTENTS #136
WINTER 2024

EAST ASIA

NONFICTION

VIỆT NAM

3   **The River Collects Its Debt** Story by Phước Tiến, translated from the Vietnamese by Nguyễn An Lý

12 **Respite** Joshua Jones in Hà Nội

25 **Cover Story: Hmong Mountain Guide** Lewis Davies

JAPAN

27 **Powder to the People! The Philosophy of Hokkaidō Capitalist Ski Bum, Jac Phillips** Susan Karen Burton

39 **The Lost Welsh Story of Lafcadio Hearn (alias Yakumo Koizumi)** W John Morgan

43 **Hi-mawari** (Blodyn yr Haul/ Sunflower) Lafcadio Hearn (alias Yakumo Koizumi)

47 **Writing Japan** Jayne Joso on the Japanese settings of recent fiction and memoir titles

FURTHER FICTION

51 **The Banana Banshee** Story by Deidre Brennan, translated from the Irish by the author

REVIEW-ESSAYS

59 **Ecological Literacy** Steven Lovatt explores recent books that seek to restore natural and cultural ecologies and recognise how the cultural nature of our landscapes is preserved in language

75 **Fantastical Doubles and Split Selves** JL George on responses to trauma in three recent novels

New Welsh Review
The Old Surgery
Cardigan SA43 1ED

www.newwelshreview.com

New Welsh Review was established in 1988 by Academi and the Association for Welsh Writing in English.

Editor:
Gwen Davies
editor.newwelshreview@gmail.com

Management Board:
David Lloyd-Owen, Niall Griffiths and Richard Davies

Patrons:
Richard S Powell and Bob Borzello

Design:
Ingleby Davies Design and Syncopated Pandemonium

Proofreading:
Steven Lovatt

Cover image: Daughter of mountain guide Giang Su; image on contents page: 'Mari Lwyd Chat', William McClure Brown, courtesy of artist's estate and School of Art Museums and Galleries, Aberystwyth University.

The contents: © The New Welsh Review Ltd and the authors

Print ISBN: 978-1-913830-28-1
eBook ISBN: 978-1-913830-29-8
ISSN: 09542116

Views expressed in *NWR* are the authors' own and do not necessarily reflect the opinions of either editor or board.

All rights reserved. No part of this publication may be reproduced, stored in a retrieval system or transmitted in any form or by any means, electronic, recorded or otherwise, without the permission of the publisher, the New Welsh Review Ltd.

Mae croeso ichi ohebu â'r golygydd yn Gymraeg.

O'r Pedwar Gwynt

DARLLEN, HOLI, HERIO

£15 y flwyddyn yn unig i ddarllen pob dim

www.pedwargwynt.cymru

THE RIVER COLLECTS ITS DEBT

STORY BY **PHƯỚC TIẾN**, TRANSLATED FROM THE VIETNAMESE BY **NGUYỄN AN LÝ**

The old man was brought to the pagoda at dawn on the fifth day. It was an autumn morning, drawn and tattered. The wind had kept still for so long that, now released to play on the eyelids of mourners, it brought with it the smell of fermented worms and insects. Those making up the cremation procession had all undergone a sleepless night. It was not far to the pagoda, but the narrow dirt path threaded all muddy below a Buddhist banner burning red in the sulfur-tinted smoke from the mourners' torches. On this same path they had come home the night before, having prepared the pyre in the cremation pit, walking between rows of combretum trees silvered in the moonlight.

The boy was in the midst of that never-ending stream of people, trailing his father and the musicians in the traditional Khmer band. He had goosebumps all over, arising not just through nervousness, but the whole atmosphere: the rhythmic chants for the deceased, the sound of the clay pot banging against the top of the flagpole. Walking beside him was a girl with reddish-brown eyes, the colour of earthworms swollen fat in the dancing firelight.

The boy had just experienced the most horrific night in his young life. He had jolted awake in the darkest hours, to see the coffin lid wide open. His grandfather, furious, was climbing out. From his chest, midriff and legs, wrapping cloths came loose. The boy had sat all curled up on the threshold, waiting in vain for the old man to call out to him. A slow rhythm, like someone hammering on a chisel, was all that reached his ears, but it was too far away to locate. Against a background of shimmering violet, the shade of those desolate twilights on the riverbank, behind the candle which had inexpicably given up the ghost, his grandfather was now hovering above the intricately decorated coffin. His stomach was a yawning cave, empty of viscera. The boy thought he glimpsed, deep inside that cave, the tattered shape of a hut, crouching beside a soaring majestic steeple. Harsh laughter escaped from the old man. Unfurling from the pole in his hand was a white Buddhist flag bearing the image of a crocodile. His laughter echoed off the smoke-stained roof beams, paralysing the boy with fear. With a sudden shriek, the old man hurled the flagpole towards him. The ground shook, quivered and split apart. From innumerable cracks, rats swarmed out, squealing in innocent delight. The boy screamed, 'No, grandfather! Please, no!'

By the time his anxious father came to wake him up, the boy had become almost mad with terror. The father clasped his son's scrawny shoulders in his strong arms. The smell of the funeral spirits he had been drinking, infused with garlic cloves, brought the child to his senses, making him weep and confide his dream. The man's face darkened. He looked up at the altar, now also tearful. The candle, which had been lit five days ago as a symbol of the deceased's kindness towards the living, was no longer burning.

On the previous day, when the level of garlic alcohol in each decanter had dropped to less than half, five men had left the funeral party and embarked on a boat. The group had included the boy, who was considered a man by now. During the harvest, he had spent many nights in a granary hut together with the girl of the earthworm-coloured eyes.

The five tanned men, glistening with strength, had taken turns to guide the boat down the shallow mud-laden stream. Then they came to the great river. A solitary hut stood on the riverbank. The owner was away, transporting sugarcanes to the dam. They'd moored their boat in front of the hut. All they had with them were some shredded tobacco leaves and a few farm tools. The men had lain scattered on the riverbank, rolling cigarette after cigarette as they waited. The days-long funeral preparation had squeezed out the last drops of energy from them. In the very first days, they had had to scour the mangrove swamps of the South in order to fuel the pyre, but had come back almost empty-handed, save for some trees too young and fresh. The previous year, the weather was so dire there'd been mass deaths, and the living had visited upon the dry mangrove forests a devastation from which they hadn't yet recovered.

Patiently, humbly, the five men had waited until high noon; five dried corkwood trees in the sun. No one rolled as many cigarettes as the boy, who felt like his throat was burning. He had heard from his father that the hut belonged to a man with brown eyes, a man from the North. Certain missteps in the war had sent him to prison, from where he'd emerged, denuded of everything but the clothes on his back. The boy's grandfather had taken pity on him. This was long before the boy became a man. That hapless man hadn't been able to pay back his debt, despite all those long years, and now his benefactor was dead.

Afternoon had come, the tobacco all run out. The five men got to their feet, one by one. They'd looked at one another, bathed in the violet desolation of that disorientating evening. Then the boy's father had taken up a hoe as a signal. They'd started on the thatching. Gourd-shaped slaughtering knives were enough to take down the fragile roof frame. But when they came to the main pillars, the flooring had to be upturned with hoes, disturbing a colony of rats under the kitchen wing. They worked quickly, wordlessly. Everything that had been dismantled was then moved into the boat, and when it was all finished, they planted on the gouged-up plot of land a bamboo pole, around the top of which was wrapped a white crocodile banner. The returning boat cut into the stream, grooves snaking lazily.

By the early hours of the fifth day, the mourners had all ended up inside the pagoda compound. The crematorium had been set up on the riverbank, logs neatly heaped in ready piles. The streams of people flowed down the paved path. The chief monk was waiting there, and beside him was another carrying a kasaya.

The master of ceremonies turned up the cloth covering the dead man's face. He had been a proud, generous man in his days. In the evening, he would sit on his doorstep and roll his cigarettes after a day in the fields.

He would stay there for a long time, staring straight ahead, and his chin was as smooth as a boy's. He had travelled his life always on the same path. Starting from those fields, those evenings on the doorstep, with not a hair on his chin, and never once a wavering of his eyes. But what was inside the coffin now was a log of meat the colour of mahogany, the tip of its swollen nose coming almost to its medial cleft. For the last five days, the chants for the peaceful passing of the soul had been carrying him, with all of an old farmer's pride, to set him gently sailing along and up to the steeple above the pagoda's main hall, untouched by the autumn winds.

On the first day when enbalming started, they had cut open the stomach and removed the entire viscera. But when it came to severing the corpse's hamstrings, they had to stop due to exhaustion, and in consideration of the monks, who had been waiting too long to commence their chanting. Now new shrouds had replaced the old, but the boy's father wouldn't let them resume the job. He had been shaken by his son's dream.

When the chanting finally ceased, the chief monk arrived. He stood under a young palm tree, cast a slow look around, the hint of a smile on his face. The descendants of the dead man in their rough cloth attire stood as silent and dusty as strands of passion vine. Weary and anticipating, their figures filled up the riverbank.

They had arrived, all those descendants, on the third day. Those who had wandered furthest from their homeland, all the way to the source of the Mekong, belonged to the second branch on the maternal line. They'd come home with their farewell gifts in a boat whose sides were painted with tiger stripes. The others had followed the dirt path, bringing with them musicians playing Khmer instruments or the Southern single-string zither. Tears were seldom part of their offering. To their fruit and kerosene and scrolls of fabric were added sacks of grain, opium and carob tea. They'd sat the whole night through on the brick yard in front of the steps, between rows of sturdy posts. Taking turns to haul hundreds of water carts through the vast expanse of dry fields, they only drank their own muddy well water mixed with sugar palm liquor. Peaceful, they'd sat side by side in the clear autumn night, the monks' intonation caught in gentle eddies around the young branches of white bamboo, the mist-shrouded steeple, the canopies of palm leaves. They were partly drowning their sorrows, partly celebrating this once-in-a-lifetime reunion, partly remembering the departed. Old folks sipped the little cups of garlic-clove spirits. Young men drank with abandon. In the morning, when the chanting was over, the monks had had to leave unhonoured, with not even a farewell from the host. They'd had to make their own way over limp, snoring corpses.

Now the head monk glanced at the cremation pit, then over to the river. In the distance, a bird was gently floating against a background of frost. His eyes glinted in eerie flashes of lightning; his mouth again curved in a smile.

The boy received the torch from the master of ceremonies and wordlessly climbed the stone steps to the crematorium. At the end of autumn, he was due to turn fifteen. After gathering the last armfuls of rice stalks from the threshing yard, he had told her his parting sad story. Ever since he'd known of such magic as is hidden in a girl and not a scarecrow, sorrows and quick anger had been disturbing his heart. Ever since he'd learned that he was the one chosen to sacrifice his youth to honour the deceased with a life of worship, he had visibly aged. In a short while, he would run to the great river, and lead the girl away, all the way to the river source. His cousins in the painted boat had told him about barren paths of sand and stone leading across the plains, to a place where your sole companions all year round would be winds which were aromatic with carob grass, with garlic-infused spirits, even with the scent of women, and of pagodas baked in the ferocious sun. It is a path worthy of a man, the boy thought. Here in his own land, children like him knew no childhood. The dirt path hidden under mud was the only path laid out before them till the end of their lives. There was never a fork in that road.

The torch travelled a short distance through the air before sinking into the cremation pit. The boy's father looked pale. He knew why the candle had been snuffed out the previous night, the boy thought. His grandfather had no longer use for that debt now, but he was intent upon recovering it, on principle. The boy didn't know whether it might benefit the dead or the living, but he did know that he himself had no need for it. And he thought his father would also understand why he had to run away.

Fire began to leap about the bottom of the pit. The boy fell onto his knees on the stone steps. Intently he gazed into the fire. Down there, the logs were crackling. Dried combretum and hummingbird tree wood quickly caught alight, and their jelly ears curled up and withered. The living had fulfilled the wishes of the deceased. The entire hut from that far-off stretch of riverbank had been arranged neatly at the bottom of the pit, and now flames were rising from the fragile timber frame.

The four monks in charge of the ceremonial scented water had finished sprinkling it. One stayed behind with the boy. He took hold of the boy's head and began to shave his hair.

The chief monk looked up to the top of the steeple. A faint stretch of dawn had just been uncovered, and the gilded tip sparkled in the sun. His pupils widened, and he smiled for the third time.

Fire burst out with a hiss; the slap of heat was followed by clouds of black smoke. Flame billowed over the mouth of the pit, and red sap spurted out of the young mangrove palms dotting the white grave cloths. The boy stood up to receive his kasaya and noticed the smell of burning opium. Eyes wide open, he hoped for a final glimpse of his grandfather. But all he could see in the inferno was darkened wisps from the shrouds, all he could hear, the hissing sound of boiling fat. He covered his eyes. Despair, a deep despair came over him. His grandfather, his stomach gaping, must be flailing around in that inferno. Letting out a heart-rending shout, the boy took flight.

The fire tenders had all been driven back by the heat. The chief monk stayed in his place, his benevolent head a blazing shape etched onto the pale blueing sky.

Desperately, the boy ran towards the riverbank. The girl had already departed, having neatly set down a tray of offerings at the feet of the master of ceremonies. She was waiting, as promised, across the field. No one gave chase, and the boy ran and ran. Heaven swirling, earth twirling, thigh-deep mud sucking, kasaya unravelling. On the silent bank. Shrubs of acanthus and nipa palms red with alum.

On this same bank, the boy used to sit with the girl on breezy mornings of past blue autumn days. Innocently they sat on the stone embankment, watching the shrimp netters threading their way amid floats of water hyacinth. Lovely dreams played in their young hearts, seeded in those nights when the troupes would come down to the village: red togas, violet robes, silver belts. The stage was to them a land of wonder, where a child who spends their whole day in the harvested fields looking for leftover grains on the stalks can put on green silky shoes at dusk and become the child of the heir apparent.

Exhaustion caught up with the boy, even before he reached the water. He fell into a great pothole and was swallowed up to his waist in the mud. He struggled to escape, but suddenly felt weightless. An iron grip was around his neck. Before he knew it, his skinny legs slid through the mud and his whole body was thrown into the air by a terrible power. He screamed out in terror. The blindingly white crocodile flag was unfurling before his eyes. He fell back to earth, nearly fainting from the pain. Beyond the mud, he saw a giant pair of legs pinning down a dinghy, and above that a muscular stomach and a chest bursting out of a worn-out shirt. He wiped his face. Mud had now come up to his chest. Blazing eyes were boring into him out of a face of hair. In the bottom of the boat, around the man, were chewed-up bits of sugarcane. The man held the funeral flag wrapped around the crushed bamboo pole. Panicked, the boy struggled in vain to get out of the muddy sand. He screamed, hoping someone up on the riverbank would hear him. He had been anticipating such an encounter. Since the previous day, his nightmare and the ruin of the hut down the river had been preying on his mind.

The man stayed still, paying no heed to the boy's screams. Not until the boy dropped down in exhaustion did he laugh: leisurely, booming, prideful and totally out of place. He hurled the pole towards the boy, and it struck deep into the mud like pent-up anger. The boy's heart drummed in his chest, and tears were now streaming down his neck. The man abruptly turned away. He pushed the dinghy into the middle of the river with one hand, parting the dense water hyacinth floats, passing the tattered weirs, and left.

The moment the funeral flag planted itself in front of the boy, the mourners on the riverbank spread out in panic. Some screamed in terror. Chunks from the coffin were spat up into the mouth of the pit on tongues of fire. The dead man shot bolt upright on his throne. His grave wrappings had all burnt out; bits of fiery flesh fell from him like fireflies. Those who remained on the stone steps hastily prostrated themselves. The boy's father, wiping his eyes, walked to the mouth of the pit; with a long iron pole, he shoved the charred skeleton back into the inferno. All because they had neglected to cut his hamstrings.

A short distance away, where the river splits into streams to irrigate the fields, the girl was bathing. Standing in water up to her breasts, she was meticulously rinsing her towel. From time to time, she would look over at the pagoda, at the thinning smoke above the palm leaves. Slowly, so slowly, she poured water from cupped hands onto her skinny neck. She waited. Her dress was draped on a thorny bush of mangrove holly up on the riverbank.

Đỗ Phước Tiến was born in 1966 and is a fiction writer. He was born in in Đà Nẵng in 1966. When his father, an officer in the South Vietnamese Army, was imprisoned at the end of the Việt Nam War in 1975, he left school to make a living as a mechanic and a transporter of rice in Saigon. He is included in the French anthology, *Terres des Ephemeres*. In English translation, he is published in the journal TRAFIKA and the anthology, *Night, Again*.

Nguyễn An Lý lives in Ho Chi Minh City. Her translations into Vietnamese include works by Margaret Atwood, Kazuo Ishiguro, JL Borges, Amos Oz, and the poetry in *The Lord of the Rings*. As an editor, she has worked on translations from Nabokov, AS Byatt, Roland Barthes, Joseph Campbell, Viet Thanh Nguyen and Liu Cixin, among others. She won English PEN Translates Awards for *Chinatown* (Tilted Axis Press, 2022) and *Elevator in Sài Gòn* (Tilted Axis Press, 2024) by Thuận, and *Water: A Chronicle* (Major Books, 2024) by Nguyễn Ngọc Tư. *Chinatown* also won the 2023 ALTA National Translation Award in Prose and was the runner-up of the 2023 TA First Translation Prize. She co-founded and co-edits the independent online *Zzz Review*.

Tŷ Newydd

Canolfan Ysgrifennu Genedlaethol Cymru
Wales' National Writing Centre

Encilion a chyrsiau ysgrifennu preswyl, mewn sawl genre gwahanol, o £275 y pen.

Residential writing courses and retreats, available in multiple genres, starting from £275 per person.

Dechreua dy bennod nesaf.
Start your next chapter.

RESPITE

JOSHUA JONES IN HÀ NỘI

Photographs on previous and following pages by Joshua Jones

My first few days in Hà Nội I spent alone, first in a hotel and then a hostel for backpackers. This was my first time flying alone, my first time outside Europe. I wanted to get to know the place, the people – even the backpacking kids, mostly white Europeans and Americans in their early twenties, who saw Việt Nam as a stopgap between travelling onwards to Thailand, Laos or Cambodia. I didn't want to be a tourist. I didn't want to get in the face of the locals either – with my camera, I only wanted to drift, to pass by, and observe quietly.

Nothing could prepare me for Hà Nội; the unforgiving heat and humidity, the constant blaring of motorcycle horns, the smell of oils for motors and for cooking. As I walked around, often feeling overwhelmed and overstimulated, I reached for a place of solitude within myself. I attempted to take pictures from within this inner sanctum, to find this inner peace within my surroundings and reflect it back. These are pictures of quiet moments; of respite from the bustling metropolis and the heat; of spaces that encourage peace and solitude, or otherwise hold an emptiness within the loud.

Joshua Jones is a queer, autistic writer and artist from Llanelli. He co-founded Dyddiau Du, a NeuroQueer art and literature space in Cardiff. His fiction and poetry have been published by *Poetry Wales*, Broken Sleep Books, *Gutter* and others. He was a Literature Wales Emerging Writer for 2023. The photographs in this sequence were taken in May 2023 as a guest of the European Literature Festival of Hà Nội, Việt Nam, supported by the British Council Wales. The connections made resulted in *Room/Ystafell/ Phòng, a* tri-lingual anthology of new work from Vietnamese and Welsh queer writers. Short-story collection *Local Fires*, his first publication of fiction, was shortlisted during 2024 for both the Dylan Thomas Prize and the Polari First Book Award.

COVER STORY: HMONG MOUNTAIN GUIDE

LEWIS DAVIES

These are the children of Giang Su. She is a mountain guide working for a hostel in the tourist season close to her village. In the wet season she will work on the intensively farmed rice terraces which dominate the wider mountain valleys. She is part of the Hmong people of northern Việt Nam, who speak their own language and have a very distinctive culture. They have been persecuted, as all minorities seem to be, but have kept hold of their own language and traditions. The Hmong have been scattered by migration and war across the borders of Việt Nam, Laos and Thailand with a further distinct diaspora predominantly in the US. Su could speak four languages but hadn't been to school past eight or nine, so couldn't read. She is a perceptive and engaged thinker and guide.

Giang Su and her two children, Sa Pa Valley, northern Việt Nam

Lewis Davies is a writer and the publishing director of Parthian Books, as well as being the publisher of *New Welsh Review* since spring 2024.

Writers' Cabin: self-led writing retreats with sauna near Machynlleth, mid Wales

Discover the writer within you...

As featured in *The Sunday Times* | Retreats start from £117 per night

Book now: www.writewithin.wales/writers-cabin
@_writewithin

POWDER TO THE PEOPLE!
THE PHILOSOPHY OF HOKKAIDŌ CAPITALIST SKI BUM, JAC PHILLIPS

SUSAN KAREN BURTON

When I exit the train station, I panic. It has taken me two days to reach this place from Tōkyō: four hours and 696 kilometres on the northbound Hayabusa Shinkansen (twenty-three kilometres of which was through an undersea tunnel), three and a half hours on the Super Hokuto limited express to Sapporo city, another hour on a 'Lilac' train, and finally one more hour on a local – one carriage, one driver, five passengers – train to the town of Furano. It is cold, it is sleeting, and there is no one here to meet me.

Ten minutes later, a white van pulls up and a man in khaki fleece and a beanie hat leaps out. 'Sorry about the mess,' says Jac Phillips as I survey a jagged pile of skis in the back. Ignoring red traffic lights, we speed along Furano's main street, an uphill slope of low-lying buildings that end at the foot of a mountain. A ski lift disappears into the mists but I can just make out one or two hardy skiers snowploughing downhill through the slush. Furano is experiencing a heat event which could signal the end of the season. But before setting out from Sapporo this morning, I had checked the forecast. It said that a temperature drop around lunchtime would result in snow later in the day. 'Awesome!' says Jac.

Jac's introduction to snow came early. His mother, a French and Spanish teacher, took the family to Europe during the school holidays. While she enjoyed the culture and the cuisine, her son immediately took to the slopes. After one year at Cardiff University, Jac – to his parents' dismay – dropped out and moved to Austria, where he trained and worked as a ski instructor and backcountry (off-piste) skiing guide. For the next five years he chased winter in Europe and New Zealand. In 2016, he arrived in Hokkaidō.

Comprising twenty-two per cent of its land area, Hokkaidō is Japan's second largest island. Originally the province of Japan's indigenous population, the Ainu, who knew their lands (Hokkaidō and surrounding islands) as Yezo (or Ezo), it was swiftly annexed by Japan in the nineteenth century in the face of Russian expansionism. In an effort to persuade the mainlanders of Honshū to settle here, the Japanese government gave away parcels of (previously Ainu) land. But Hokkaidō's inhospitable climate deterred many. Today only five per cent (5.7 million) of the Japanese population call Hokkaidō home and, after being physically stuffed into trains in Tōkyō, I find the empty roads disconcerting.

Hokkaidō in the summer is pleasantly cool. North of North Korea and only forty-three kilometres from Russia, the island – unlike the rest of Japan – lacks humidity and a rainy season. Also unlike the rest of Japan, Hokkaidō has green grass on which cows graze to supply the country with wagyū beef and creamy, vanilla-flavoured milk. With a summer temperature in the mid twenties, Hokkaidō is a retreat for frazzled urbanites escaping the heat and humidity of Japan's sub-tropical climate. Visitors can hike in the mountain ranges, go white water rafting on the rivers, and visit wineries, farms and colourful flower meadows reminiscent of the tulip fields in Holland. If they bring a wetsuit, they can even surf.

But in winter, the temperature plummets and the island is transformed by snow. Between November and April, upwards of fifteen metres of it covers the mountain ranges, many of which are volcanically active. The capital city of Sapporo, the second snowiest city in the world, holds an annual festival where international teams compete to create the most spectacular ice sculptures. Hokkaidō snow is considered to be the best in the world, and

Jac moved to Hokkaidō because he wanted to experience it for himself. His immediate reaction was, 'This is Mecca.'

'What's so good about it?' I ask suspiciously, looking out of the van window at heaps of the stuff piled high on pavements and in car parks. Surely snow is ice water everywhere in the world. Apparently not. Japanese snow is formed by a meteorological phenomenon caused by bitter Siberian winds blowing down across the warm Sea of Japan, sucking up the moisture and creating giant clouds. When these clouds reach land, they cluster over the Japanese mountains and, as they rise up over the peaks (a movement known as orographic lift), they cool and release huge amounts of a powder snow known as 'Japow'.

Japow falls over the mountains all across Japan. Honshū has a volcanic spine which stretches from the north to the centre of the mainland, encompassing three distinct mountain areas known collectively as the Japanese Alps. Skiing and snowboarding are popular winter pastimes, and the major Honshū resorts – Hakuba, Shiga Kōgen and Nozawa Onsen – are only three hours from Tōkyō by train, close enough for weekend getaways. But it is worth venturing further north, says Jac, because the Japow in Hokkaidō is deeper and more consistent. When Jac realised he wanted to make ski instructing and guiding his career, he briefly considered New Zealand but ruled it out because recent winters have been blighted by warm, wet weather caused by climate change. Hokkaidō has so far remained unaffected by the fluctuations in temperature that have ruined ski seasons elsewhere in the world. Consequently, the snowpack – fallen snow that is compressed and hardened by its own weight – is thicker and safer in Hokkaidō. Avalanches are less likely here than on Honshū, where the temperature is a few degrees warmer. Winter temperatures in Hokkaidō hover around minus five degrees Celsius (but can drop into the minus twenties) and the slopes are continuously blanketed in soft, fresh snowfalls.

Jac began ski instructing in the town of Niseko, on the western side of the island in the Annupuri mountain range. Gathered around the slopes of Mount Niseko Annupuri (1,308 metres), Niseko United is a collective of four interconnected resorts offering sixty-one ski runs and twelve terrain parks. Back in the nineties, as Japan fell into recession, ski resorts lost money. The Niseko Hanazono resort was purchased by a group of Australian investors, and Qantas-owned Australian Airlines began twice-weekly ski season flights into Sapporo. With basic facilities and an undeveloped terrain, the resort was a big hit with Aussie snowboarders.

But in recent years, new faces have appeared on the piste, the wealthy citizens of the burgeoning Asian economies: mainland Chinese (often British educated and carrying American passports), Hong Kong Chinese, Singaporeans and Malaysians. As the French Alps are to the British middle classes, so Niseko has developed as the premier winter vacation destination for the Asian nouveau riche. Jac estimates that around three-quarters of the ski tourists in Niseko are foreign, wealthy and highly educated.

In Niseko, well-heeled vacationers like to spend their money. They demand five-star accommodation: at the Ritz Carlton, the Park Hyatt or their own luxury chalets. They eat only the freshest Hokkaidō sushi at the resort's fifteen Michelin-starred or recommended restaurants. And they require ski instructors on call who can offer lessons in the global elite's common language, English. Some of the über rich have skied all their lives, others are beginners, Asia having no traditional ski culture. And not everyone wants ski lessons. Jac admits he sometimes acts solely as a sherpa, carrying equipment. Or else he will drive them to the slopes so they can pose in designer gear to show off on Instagram. Jac has sometimes sat for hours in hotel receptions, not knowing if his clients will appear or if he will simply be paid off and told to come back tomorrow. But there are perks. Tipping is not the custom in Japan but in Niseko a foreign culture prevails, with a wad of cash in the hand at the end of the day. Instructors who introduce clients to local restaurants can also find themselves seated at their table, enjoying a free meal. As long as they don't join the conversation. 'You're there to sit and be quiet,' warns Jac.

After nine winters (Jac counts in units of seasons), he and British wife Makenzie (who he met in Austria) moved over to Furano. The resort sits in the dead centre, or belly button, of Hokkaidō and the locals celebrate this fact with an annual belly button festival, painting happy faces on their torsos and donning low straw hats. Compared to Niseko, Furano remains relatively unknown and undeveloped, and I wonder why the couple would relocate away from a major client base to a rural outpost which even Jac describes as 'a farming town with a ski hill'. 'There is more opportunity over here in Furano,' he says, parking the van. 'I thought I'd get a foothold in.'

In late 2019, Jac and Makenzie founded their own ski business, Summit (summitski.jp). They have recently opened a shop and office, conveniently located at the base of the resort's main ski slope. Inside, the walls are lined with skis and snowboards for sale and for rent. With hot coffees in hand, Jac and his office manager, Gabil, list Furano's attractions.

Furano, begins Jac, has the deepest snow he has ever encountered. At high season, two months of whiteout is not unusual. In the mornings, Jac shovels half a metre of it from his driveway to get the van out and the same amount again to park it at night. Consequently, with fewer people on Furano's runs, there is still powder aplenty after lunch when Niseko is skied out.

The snow is also drier. Dry snow is formed in colder temperatures. Also known as champagne snow, it creates optimum conditions for skiing or snowboarding, giving a feeling of floating over the terrain rather than slicing through it. 'The product is powder, and you want to deliver the product,' Jac points out.

But the biggest draw for Jac is not Furano's curated ski fields but its hinterland. Furano borders the largest national park in Japan, Daisetsuzan, home to Hokkaidō's highest mountains, a range of eight dormant strato-volcanoes situated in an actively volcanic landscape. It is a vast, unexplored wilderness of steep fir- and birch-covered slopes, frozen creeks and even the odd steaming fumarole. It offers 'rocky, craggy' skiing and the excitement of plunging down narrow chutes and near-vertical couloirs (seams or fissures in the mountainside). 'It's some of the craziest terrain I've ever seen,' says Jac with a grin. There are even opportunities for 'first ascents', to ski where no one has skied before.

Backcountry skiing is a relatively new phenomenon in Japan, where ski resorts are highly regulated. On groomed slopes, resort operators feel they can control everything. Off-piste is labelled 'abunai' (dangerous). Accidents suggest a resort is badly managed and Japanese skiers will go elsewhere. 'They don't like risk,' says Gabil. 'They like being safe.'

Japan's collectivist culture promotes social harmony and rewards conformity. Its citizens will not inconvenience those around them by breaking the rules. Japanese skiers stay within the ropes and keep to the approved trails and runs. 'For some reason, Japanese love being cordoned off,' Jac explains with a frown. In other countries, he points out, it is down to the individual to look after themselves, to decide whether they have the knowledge and experience to venture off supervised trails. And when foreigners come to the Japanese ski fields and see virgin snow on the other side of the ropes, they duck them, heading off-piste and disappearing into the trees. Recently, Japanese operators have begun bowing to the inevitable, establishing a gate system which allows access to areas that are not completely groomed.

Backcountry is extreme skiing and not without risk. The previous month, three foreigners had died in avalanches on Japan's off-piste slopes, two in Hakuba and one near Niseko. 'It *is* dangerous out there,' agrees Jac. Which is why Hokkaidō needs experienced guides. Japanese guides do not always have the expertise required to take clients off-piste. Qualified as a backcountry guide, a wilderness first responder (equipped to handle medical emergencies in remote locations) and trained in avalanche risk management, Jac has that expertise. He understands the local terrain and the weather conditions. Avalanches are 'the dragon you play with', he warns. 'But if it goes well, it's a lot of fun.'

In hindsight, winter 2019–20 was the worst time to start a business. Although under constitutional law the Japanese government was unable to enforce a Covid pandemic lockdown, gatherings were discouraged, and locals took to checking car number plates (which display the prefecture in which they were registered) for signs of out-of-towners. When Japan closed its national borders, resort hotels emptied and Hokkaidō's foreign-directed tourism industry all but collapsed. Now the tourists have returned and Summit is enjoying a busy season, welcoming not only the super-rich Asians but also French, Italians, Swiss, Scandinavians, Kiwis, Australians and Americans who want to spend their holidays ripping up the powder. Summit has taken on two office staff and several ski instructors, and is looking to recruit a Chinese speaker.

Summit provides a concierge service tailored to each client's desire, be it skiing (day or night), backcountry exploration, photographic or film-making tours (popular with Americans who like to make Hollywood-style ski movies), onsen (hot springs) trips, sightseeing and even visits to local festivals. 'We're not just a numbers game,' states Jac. 'We take pride in what we do.' The company maintains a foothold in Niseko but in Furano it caters to the powder hounds, adventurous skiers who travel the globe seeking that next white powder high.

After ski-bumming for a decade and living on seasonal salaries plus tips, Jac wants to monetise his (and Makenzie's) experience and expertise. He is fortunate, he says, that Makenzie is organised. 'She's the operations manager,' chips in Gabil. Jac has the big ideas, Makenzie figures out how to make them happen. 'It's weird because now I've turned into a capitalist ski bum,' says Jac, laughing hysterically as we climb back into the van.

As we head out of town, we pass vacant lots with signboards announcing the imminent construction of modern condo-hotels, opulent chalets and managed villas, top-end real estate that will soon replace the old minshuku, traditional Japanese guesthouses. Foreign developers are moving in, keen to buy into the lucrative luxury Hokkaidō tourist business. 'Furano is just kicking off,' says Jac. I wonder out loud what Furano locals think about new-comers, and Jac admits they are wary. Having seen the Aussies in Niseko (whom he likens to the British in Spain) they have become 'leery', and complain that there's more talk of money than there is of skiing. 'They're scared we won't uphold their values or morals,' he adds. He acknowledges the paradox of encouraging foreign skiers to ditch the Niseko tourist trap and follow him to Furano. It is only a matter of time before Furano's slopes fill up. 'But for the time being there's powder in abundance for everyone,' he says.

Over lunch (in a renovated wooden farm shed – one of those places that only locals know) Jac lays out his strategy for Summit in Furano. He plans to offer a unique adventure to clients: to take them out into the wilderness of the backcountry – initially on snowmobiles but later in snowcats and even heliskiing – to hike in nature, to encounter herds of wild deer and to ski in waist-deep snow. The terrain around Furano is 'raw' and undeveloped, and he wants more people to enjoy it. 'I want to bring powder to the people,' he announces with a wide grin.

Before we head into Daisetsuzan National Park, we make a stop at Jac and Makenzie's home in the village of Nunobe. When we arrive, my first thought is that the couple has been robbed. The front door is wide open. Then two giant Akita dogs, large as bears and just as hairy, appear in the doorway, blinking curiously through the sleet. The house, a former akiya, was once the village shop and the front, which used to be the shopfloor, is left open for Nalu and Griff. The living area is in the back. Constructed in the eighties, like most Japanese homes it is made of wood. Wooden houses are expected to last no more than thirty to forty years and, when adult children inherit their parents' property, they generally knock down the old and build new. 'Japanese like new stuff,' says Jac. 'They even teach in schools that your electrical kitchen appliances should be renewed every three years.' But like most akiya buyers I have met, Jac and Makenzie are in the process of renovating. As the walls are too thin to insulate, Jac has fixed cladding to the outside. Much in the same way as many Japanese place new rugs over old, he is adding layers to keep in the warmth. And to stop the water pipes freezing.

Inside, they heat the traditional Japanese way, with kerosene. Kerosene heaters are smelly and greasy and liable to singe your eyebrows off if you get too close, but the oil doesn't freeze in low temperatures. The heat, however, does not reach everywhere. The house has a unit bathroom, a metal capsule containing a shower, bath and basin. In winter, Jac admits, it's like washing inside an ice cube.

Jac feeds his dogs. Nalu and Griff are oblivious to the driving sleet. In fact, they seem to enjoy it. Akita are hardy animals with a strong prey drive. They recently disappeared for four days, chasing wild deer in the mountains, and returned none the worse. This morning, from the window of the local train, I had seen numerous deer tracks tracing around white birch trees, the bark stripped. Deer numbers are increasing because Japan's ageing human population means there are fewer hunters left with the energy to trek into the mountains to find them. But the deer have other predators. Hokkaidō is home to the Ussuri or Ezo brown bear, a near relative of the grizzly and almost as big. There are estimated to be between three and fifteen thousand bears living in Hokkaidō's remote and environmentally protected wilderness and, as hunting them is prohibited, they are becoming braver, wandering into towns and attacking the locals. Northern Hokkaidō is the scene of Japan's most notorious bear attack. In 1915, in the village of Sankebetsu, a nearly nine-foot-tall Ezo bear killed seven residents in less than a week.

Recently, while out driving on one of the nearby forest trails, Jac encountered a giant Ezo bear, its rump higher than the bonnet of the car he was rapidly reversing. He had earlier come across scattered deer legs while walking his dogs, and his close encounter was followed by a note through his letterbox warning Nunobe residents that a mother and cub were using the village as a short cut to reach a nearby river.

Deer and bears aside, Jac and Makenzie assumed their rural life would be quiet. At Nunobe's tiny station, the train stops only four times a day. But when tour buses began arriving, they discovered that the village was a place of pilgrimage for viewers of a long-running Fuji television series, *Kita no Kuni Kara* (From a Northern Country) about the idyllic rural life of a divorced man who returns with his two children to his hometown. 'We need to open a tea shop,' announces Jac.

Nunobe is a village with a dwindling number of elderly residents. The previous occupant of Jac and Makenzie's home was a ninety-year-old woman who moved to a retirement complex. But Jac and Makenzie are not the only foreigners in the area. Their neighbour, and some time employee, is also Welsh. Later, I chat with him on Zoom.

John Llywelyn arrived in Hokkaidō in 2019. He learned to ski on the dry slopes of Llandudno, and instructed there while he was in the sixth form. After five years in the merchant navy, he worked winter seasons in Canada and New Zealand before arriving in Japan. 'That's the next step,' he explains. 'If you've done North America and you don't want to do Europe, then you go east to Japan.' He had no problem finding a job. He estimates there are over a thousand foreign instructors in Hokkaidō during the winter season.

During the Covid pandemic, other instructors left the country but John had just married his Japanese wife. He found work in a food processing factory, sorting and bagging onions from local farms. The couple bought a house near Jac and Makenzie's because it was cheap (2.7 million yen: £13,196, which they paid for in cash) and convenient, although it doesn't have mains sewage.

Another outdoors type, John loves Hokkaidō: skiing, white water rafting (which he teaches in the summer), driving up into the mountains to soak in the onsen. 'It's beautiful,' he says. 'I can't recommend it enough.' It even reminds him of Wales. 'I tell people I live in the Anglesey of Japan. Because it's not densely populated, just little villages and farms everywhere. Nobody knows about it.' As Jac's van pulls away, we pass John's house. It is shut up and Jac doesn't think John has visited in a long time. 'He's bought a bar in Niseko,' he says, sadly. 'For the après-ski.'

By the time we arrive at the summit of Mount Tokachi (2,077 metres), one of the eight active volcanoes in Daisetsuzan national park, the sleet has whipped itself into a blizzard. A tractor and a giant snowblower are attempting to clear the car park but are dwarfed by the height of the snow around them. I slither across a road glazed with ice, trying to take photographs, my hair freezing to my forehead. But Jac stands happily on the edge of a sheer drop and, as the storm rages around him, smokes a cigarette. He's not even wearing a coat. In his element, he is eager to share his thoughts, shouting over the howl of the wind. When he was younger, he says, he always 'hiked to ride', meaning he sought the shortest walking distance in order to find the longest ski line. Impatient to ski, he considered it boring to walk in nature. Now that he is older, he confesses that hiking has become a pilgrimage. Spending time in nature has become a meditation for him. It is in these mountains that he encounters his 'Zen monk' moments, and in the backcountry that he finds peace. He frowns, struggling to explain. 'I don't know if I'm doing it justice.' Lost for the right words, he pulls out his smartphone and shows me a video of a giant stag he encountered on a recent hike in the Daisetsuzan wilderness. Its tree-like antlers shudder as it leaps along a frozen creek bed and dives through the snow, fearful of Jac's camera. But when the stag realises he is in no danger he stops, and the watcher becomes the watched. 'Awesome,' says Jac.

Prompted, he admits that he misses Wales and Llanharan, his hometown. But on his last visit home, he felt estranged from Welsh-speaking friends and detected an animosity over his decision to leave, as if his departure was a rejection of the country. His experience echoes that of other interviewees [of the author's forthcoming book, *The Transplantable Roots of Catharine Huws Nagashima: Encounters with the Welsh in Japan*] who went home and found they no longer belonged. Jac doesn't see himself going back. 'What would I do there?' he muses. Jac is one of those people who must always be in motion. As skateboarders seek the smoothest concrete, and surfers live for the perfect wave, skiers like Jac pursue that perfect line: the steepest, most exhilarating downhill run. He knows it sounds 'dudeish' but he doesn't care. 'There's a beautiful line that does exist,' he says, making it sound mythical. 'And that's what I'm chasing.'

Descending the mountain, we speed across the flat expanse of Furano Valley. I gaze out of the window at the undulating white fields and the occasional farmhouse with a snowblower parked in the driveway. In early summer, when the snow turns to rain, it will refresh the soil, and these fields will bloom with rows of lavender, tulips, zinnia, marigolds, dahlias, pansies, irises and sunflowers. Giant striped beach towels of colour. 'Have you ever driven this fast before?' Jac asks. I look at the speedometer. He's doing 125 kilometres an hour. Through a blizzard. With all the skis sliding around in the back. But the road is flat and there are no other cars. 'The speed limits round here are a joke,' he says and puts his foot down. Jac Phillips is an adrenaline junkie. And a white powder addict. But he is also a backcountry pilgrim, seeking meditative moments of peace in a harsh mountain wilderness. Very dudeish.

Two hours and two trains later I am back in Sapporo city, inhaling a steaming bowl of miso ramen noodles and enjoying the restaurant's free wifi. Consulting a weather website, I see that the temperature has dropped rapidly and snow is falling again in Furano. The ski season is not yet over. Awesome!

This is a preview extract chapter from *The Transplantable Roots of Catharine Huws Nagashima: Encounters with the Welsh in Japan*, a book originally conceived for the New Welsh Rarebyte imprint established by *New Welsh Review*, and forthcoming from Parthian on 1 March, 2025.

Susan Karen Burton is an oral historian with an interest in creative nonfiction. She was born in Scotland, raised in New Zealand and spent most of her working life in Japan. There, like many of the interviewees in her forthcoming book, she began her career as a Japan Exchange and Teaching (JET) Programme assistant language teacher (ALT) in Hamamatsu, Shizuoka prefecture. She was later a Ministry of Education, Culture, Sports, Science and Technology (MEXT) scholar at Tsuda Juku University in Tōkyō. After gaining her doctorate in history from the University of Sussex, she lectured in Japanese universities for ten years before returning to the UK to do a second PhD, this time in creative and critical writing at the University of East Anglia. She won the New Welsh Writing Awards 2020 Rheidol Prize for Prose with a Welsh Theme or Setting for an early chapter from *The Transplantable Roots of Catharine Huws Nagashima*.

THE LOST WELSH STORY OF LAFCADIO HEARN (ALIAS YAKUMO KOIZUMI)

W JOHN MORGAN

LAFCADIO HEARN (1850–1904) WAS ONE OF THE OUTSTANDING interpreters of Japanese culture for an Occidental readership. He was born on the Greek Ionian Island of Lefkada on 27 June, 1850, the son of Charles Bush Hearn, an Anglo–Irish medical officer in the British Army, and Rosa Cassimati, a Greek of humble family. Lafcadio Hearn had an unsettled childhood in Ireland as the ward of his paternal great aunt Sarah Brenane, whose family also owned a house near Bangor in north Wales. As a young man of nineteen, Hearn emigrated to the United States, working as a journalist in Cincinnati, New Orleans, and later moved to the French West Indies. In 1890, he went to Japan where he settled, marrying Setsuko Koizumi, with whom he had four children.

Lafcadio Hearn is now celebrated for his retelling of Japanese folktales and acute interpretative comments on culture, religion, and natural history, written originally under the pen name of Yakumo Koizumi. Hearn's accounts of a traditional Japan on the cusp of modernisation were enhanced by a keen intellect, a scholarship marked by humility and care, a poetic imagination and clarity of style. Although criticised as a romantic by some Western academics, Hearn was respected, and indeed loved by Japanese colleagues. On Hearn's death, the poet Yone Noguchi said of him, 'Truly he was a delicate, easily broken Japanese vase, old as the world, beautiful as a cherry blossom. Alas! That wonderful vase was broken. He is no more with us.' (Hearn, 1908, 17.) Examples of Hearn's writings are the classic *Glimpses of Unfamiliar Japan* (1976), published first in 1894, and the collections *In Ghostly Japan* (1971) and *Kwaidan: Stories and Studies of Strange Things* (1927), first published in 1904. The last was the inspiration for a Japanese film of the same name directed by Masaki Kobayashi in 1964. There are also biographies, notably *Paul Murray's A Fantastic Journey: The Life and Literature of Lafcadio Hearn* (1993).

Less well known is that one of the stories in the *Kwaidan* collection is set in north Wales, where Hearn spent holidays as a lonely and impressionable young child. This is 'Hi-mawari' (Blodyn yr Haul/Sunflower), the story of a brief encounter between the child Lafcadio, his admired friend, Robert, and an itinerant Welsh harper, perhaps an individual of Romany background, that had a long-lasting emotional effect on the writer. The story is influenced by the ethics of Japanese aesthetics, and as in haiku: 'To do what a painter endeavours to do with a few strokes of the brush – to evoke an image or a mood – to revive a sensation or an emotion.' (Hearn, 1997, 154).

Hearn's ethical purpose is seen in the final paragraph. It is known that Robert later became a Merchant Navy officer and died attempting to save a fellow seaman. John Moran (2015) claims the incident with the harper took place at Strandhill in Ireland, that Lafcadio Hearn's playmate was his cousin (Robert Elwood), the harper, the local man, Dan Fitzpatrick. The latter's song, well known at the time, includes the lines, 'As the sunflower turns to her god when he sets / The same look which she turned when he rose'. The song was a favourite of Catherine, Robert's mother. Moran does not suggest why Hearn set the story in Wales and indeed doesn't refer to this at all. Nor did Hearn's biographer Paul Murray. In the Introduction to *Kwaidan*, written in Tokyo on 20 January, 1904, Hearn did not explain why his story became a Welsh one or why he included it in the *Kwaidan* collection. The story is, I believe, virtually unknown in Wales, which is why it is offered here.

Further Reading
Lafcadio Hearn, *Kwaidan: Stories and Studies of Strange Things* (The Travellers' Library, Jonathan Cape, 1927).
Lafcadio Hearn, *In Ghostly Japan* (Charles E Tuttle Company, 1971).
Lafcadio Hearn, *Glimpses of Unfamiliar Japan* (Charles E Tuttle Company, 1976).
John Moran, 'Some Early Influences on Lafcadio Hearn' in *The Green Book: Writings on Irish Gothic, Supernatural and Fantastic Literature*, No 6 (Samhain, 2015), pp20-40.
Paul Murray, *A Fantastic Journey: The Life and Literature of Lafcadio Hearn* (Japan Library, Sandgate, 1993).

W John Morgan is Professor Emeritus, School of Education, University of Nottingham; and Leverhulme Emeritus Fellow, Wales Institute of Economic and Social Research and Data, Cardiff University.

The Borzello Trust Poetry Prize

Submit your poems by the 31st of January 2025!

We're thrilled to announce a new poetry category in the 10th year of the New Welsh Writing Awards – thanks to generous support from the Borzello Trust!

We're looking for six original and unpublished poems, with one poem exploring the theme of 'Welsh Churchyards'.

Submit your poetry to win a £500 poetry development publishing contract. There will also be a £150 cash-prize & publication for 5 highly commended entries.

For full details and competition terms scan here or visit newwelshreview.com

PARTHIAN

HI-MAWARI
(BLODYN YR HAUL/SUNFLOWER)

LAFCADIO HEARN (ALIAS YAKUMO KOIZUMI)

On the wooded hill behind the house Robert and I are looking for fairy-rings. Robert is eight years old, comely, and very wise – I am a little more than seven – and I reverence Robert. It is a glowing glorious August day; and the warm air is filled with sharp sweet scents of resin.

We do not find any fairy-rings; but we find a great many pine-cones in the high grass.... I tell Robert the old Welsh story of the man who went to sleep, unawares, inside a fairy-ring, and so disappeared for seven years, and would never eat or speak after his friends had delivered him from the enchantment.

'They eat nothing but the points of needles, you know,' says Robert.

'Who?' I ask.

'Goblins,' Robert answers. This revelation leaves me dumb with astonishment and awe.... But Robert suddenly cries out, 'There is a harper! – He is coming to the house!'

And down the hill we run to hear the harper.... But what a harper! Not like the hoary minstrels of the picture books. A swarthy, sturdy, unkempt vagabond, with black bold eyes under scowling black brows. More like a bricklayer than a bard, – and his garments are corduroy!

'Wonder if he is going to sing in Welsh?' murmurs Robert.

I feel too much disappointed to make any remarks.

The harper poses his harp – a huge instrument – upon our doorstep, sets all the strings ringing with a sweep of his grimy fingers, clears his throat with a sort of angry growl, and begins –

Believe me, if all those endearing young charms,
Which I gaze on so fondly to-day....

The accent, the attitude, the voice, all fill me with repulsion unutterable, – shock me with a new sensation of formidable vulgarity. I want to cry out loud, 'You have no right to sing that song!' For I have heard it sung by the lips of the dearest and fairest being in my little world; – and that this rude, coarse man should dare to sing it vexes me like a mockery, – angers me like an insolence.

But only for a moment! With the utterance of the syllables 'to-day', that deep, grim voice suddenly breaks into a quivering tenderness indescribable; – then, marvellously changing, it mellows into tones sonorous and rich as the bass of a great organ, – while a sensation unlike anything ever felt before takes me by the throat.... What witchcraft has he learned? What secret has he found – this scowling man of the road?... Oh! Is there anybody else in the whole world who can sing like that?... And the form of the singer flickers and dims; – and the house, and the lawn, and all visible shapes of things tremble and swim before me. Yet instinctively I fear that man; – I almost hate him; and I feel myself flushing with anger and shame because of his power to move me thus....

'He made you cry,' Robert compassionately observes, to my further confusion, – as the harper strides away, richer by a gift of sixpence taken without thanks.... 'But I think he must be a gipsy. Gipsies are bad people – and they are wizards.... Let us go back to the wood.'

We climb again to the pines, and there squat down upon the sun-flecked grass, and look over town and sea. But we do not play as before: the spell of the wizard is strong upon us both....

'Perhaps he is a goblin,' I venture at last, 'or a fairy?'

'No,' says Robert, 'only a gipsy. But that is nearly as bad. They steal children, you know.'

'What shall we do if he comes up here?' I gasp, in sudden terror at the lonesomeness of our situation.

'Oh, he wouldn't dare,' answers Robert, 'not by daylight, you know.'

*

[Only yesterday, near the village of Takata, I noticed a flower which the Japanese call by nearly the same name as we do: Hi-mawari, 'The Sunward-turning' – and over the space of forty years, there thrilled back to me the voice of that wandering harper, –

As the Sunflower turns on her god, when he sets,
The same look that she turned when he rose.

Again I saw the sun-flecked shadows on that far Welsh hill; and Robert for a moment again stood beside me, with his girl's face and his curls of gold. We were looking for fairy-rings.... But all that existed of the real Robert must long ago have suffered a sea-change into something rich and strange.... Greater love hath no man than this, that a man lay down his life for his friend. ...]

Lafcadio Hearn (1850–1904) was one of the outstanding interpreters of Japanese culture for an Occidental readership.

The Rheidol Prize—Call for Entries

The Rheidol Prize for Prose with a Welsh Theme or Setting has championed new voices and the development of writers for the past ten years, with thanks to the generous support of RS Powell in recent years. We are delighted to continue the prize this year calling for entries of new fiction and prose writing up to **5,000 words in length.**

Open to new and established writers based in the UK, as well as writers from across the globe if they have been educated in Wales for a minimum of six months.

Competition closes for entries on the 31st of January 2025. Good luck!

For full eligibility and prize conditions please scan here or visit newwelshreview.com

The Rheidol Prize
for Prose with a Welsh Theme or Setting

WRITING JAPAN

JAYNE JOSO ON THE JAPANESE SETTINGS OF RECENT FICTION
AND MEMOIR TITLES

THE ROLES OF FICTION AND MEMOIR CAN BE CURIOUSLY SIMILAR IN their ability to transport the reader to a place and sense of otherness, and it is interesting for me to reflect on this idea in my fiction on Japan, *My Falling Down House* and *Japan Stories* alongside Eluned Gramich's wonderful memoir of living in Hokkaido, *Woman Who Brings the Rain*. For what does it mean to write about a culture, a place, and people, other than your own?

The first element to consider is perhaps that of desire or motivation. What takes the writer abroad? What makes the writer set up home there? The simple answer might be curiosity, the need for a change of environment and inspiration, and the desire just as much, to be away from what you are used to. But does that make it acceptable to write at length about the new places that you inhabit and their people? I would always argue that doing just that is essential for the writer with a somewhat nomadic instinct. However else might we appreciate the difficulties of the lives of others or open up to learning often more intelligent ways of approaching life? And if we do not write about these, we are failing to share this discourse with readers. And it needs to be the discourse of many writers, in many forms, shared broadly, and rightly debated as much as enjoyed. But what is certain is that the engagement with another culture, whether fictionally or through journalism or memoir, is perhaps what Martha Nussbaum describes as an invitation for both writers and readers 'to put themselves in the place of people of many different kinds', and that through reading we can appreciate 'what is it like to live the life of another person who might, given changes in circumstance, be oneself.' I think this can also be applied to landscape and culture – what if this other scenery was the view I had grown up with, what if the land I lived upon shook with earthquakes just as it does here? What must it have been like to live always in a house made of wood with paper sliding doors? What if I had always eaten sweet persimmon as a child?

In Eluned Gramich's memoir of her time in Hokkaido, I am touched by this scene between the writer and her host family:

> *'Ame-onna,' says Kuniko, smiling. 'Rain girl. We never had so much rain before you came. The rain follows you wherever you go.'*
> *'Well, I'm from Wales.'*

What seems to happen in this brief exchange is that as the reader, you are thrust into this very particular culture, experienced through the mention of unfamilar words, 'ame-onna, rain girl' along with the sense that it is actually possible for someone to influence the weather, and at the same time, the reader is transported back to Wales with the reference that the rain is also heavy in that part of the world. Connections are made, and empathy moves from writer to Japanese host family, and back to a rainy Wales through the reader.

Later in her memoir, Gramich draws connections between her own past, and her current situation in Japan and a calligraphy class:

> *A long time ago at school, I learnt that in Islam, there's no point attending prayers if you're distracted or if you're lacking in good intentions. You must be in the right frame of mind before you even enter the mosque, before washing your feet and hands, before settling down to pray. Similarly, you should be focussed and calm before you take your calligraphy brush in hand. You should be filled with good intentions.*

The layering of knowledge and experiences here is wonderful. And Gramich moves us geographically, culturally and philosophically between Wales and

Japan, between the practice of Islamic prayer and that of Japanese calligraphy, and all in one brief paragraph.

In the novel, *My Falling Down House*, I wrote the main character, Takeo Tanaka, in the first person. He is a young Japanese guy, I am a middle-aged English woman. How could I do that? Isn't that cultural appropriation? It's an interesting topic, certainly. But I feel that if an elderly Canadian man wrote a truthful portrayal of an English (or indeed Welsh) woman, I would not mind in the least. And in contrast, if an English woman wrote such a novel, but did not write well, and did not address the life and experiences truthfully, then I would rather she had not. What I think is required of a writer, is that they are true to the subject they have chosen, that it is clear that they have done the research, that they have the breadth of life experience and emotional capacity to render the characters and situations with fictional integrity. Honestly, I don't mind where you come from.

George Eliot in her essay *The Natural History of German Life* (1895) addresses just how literature can convey the events and expression of someone else's life,

> *It is a mode of amplifying experience and extending our contact with our fellow-men beyond the bounds of our personal lot.*

Perhaps then, writing has always been this way of communicating both our own lives and those of others. In his book, *The Deliverance of Others*, David Palumbo-Liu discusses how literature 'demands both identifictation and difference at once,' and how 'we find a vacillating dynamic between empathy and critique, sameness and difference, that creates in the texts I examine a particular image of what it is to live with others in the contemporary world.'

It seems reasonable to say that the intention is not entirely to come to understand and align whilst reading, but rather to appreciate and acknowledge similarities and diversity, to bring cultures other than our own into our realm of knowledge and to place them along with our own lives under scrutiny.

And so, with my years of living in both rural Niigata prefecture and then in Tokyo, I decided, like a method actor, to play the part of a young Japanese man. Takeo is twenty-five and has lost his job, his home and his girlfriend. Initially, he takes refuge in a box under a table at work, and later in one of Japan's many abandoned traditional houses.

> *Strange to think that this series of events now positioned me as little more than a criminal....*
>
> *My life had become too slippery and, like a sweet, sticky ball of rice, once it fell it simply gathered more and more mess. A man, when he falls, first becomes a box man, and next a sticky ball of rice. It's not a good way for things to go.*

It interests me that though styles of writing differ, author to author, and between various forms of writing: memoir, fiction writing and journalism, something holds true to them all, and that is the requirement of authenticity. Perhaps I should say for the case of fiction, at least the appearance of authenticity – for here is a man who has never existed but who, on the page and in our imagination, is hopefully real and true.

Notes

Woman Who Brings the Rain: A Memoir of Hokkaido, Japan by Eluned Gramich, winner of the New Welsh Writing Awards 2015, was published this spring in a new edition by Parthian.

Jayne Joso is the author of the Japan-inspired novels, *My Falling Down House* (Seren, 2016) and *Japan Stories* (Seren, 2021).

THE BANANA BANSHEE

STORY BY **DEIDRE BRENNAN**, TRANSLATED FROM THE IRISH
BY THE AUTHOR

Anyone watching would have sworn I was giving Val my undivided attention. My friend Fidelma, an inveterate matchmaker, had just introduced us. Her choice of men for me usually left me cold and this was no exception. I was actually drifting in and out of listening as if I was coming out of an anaesthetic. The evening was a bit of a yawn and it took all my willpower not to retreat into myself, to ponder the futility of life and to count stars shooting against the velvety darkness of my brain. Val's voice jolted me back like a dig in the ribs.

'Did you know that it was the Pilgrim Fathers themselves who invented it?'

What on earth was he on about?

'I'm telling you now. They used to make a concoction of pine needles and the chippings of walnut trees. Oh yes. The cocktail's sure come a long way!'

I laughed with relief. Encouraged, he leaned closer towards me.

'Here, have a slurp of my Alabama Fog-cutter. It's the drop of vermouth that makes the difference.'

The idea of a cocktail hour had been dreamed up by Fidelma as a fund-raiser for the local musical society, trying to recoup losses on its most recent production *Hello Dolly*. She had modelled the evening on the Plaza Hotel, New York in the 1930s, which was why I was standing there, all six feet of me, *gottied* up in short black silk, ballooning out in layers of fringed chiffon and thinking only of escape.

'So, what are you drinking?'

Wow! There was actually a gap in his knowledge!

'Banana Banshee,' I said sourly, licking what tasted like a lemony-orange froth from my lips.

'Can I have a taste?'

I handed him my swizzle stick knowing he couldn't possibly taste much.

'Mmmmm...,' he sucked, 'nice tension there between the ingredients.'

He scanned me up and down. He had an aquiline nose that gave him a greedy look as if he wanted to possess me. In what sense I wasn't sure, but I had these vibes that lodged somewhere in my guts. I clung to my glass as if it were a strong stake anchoring me.

'What do you do?' Val questioned.

'I'm an artist,' I said evasively.

'Me too.'

'What kind?'

'Oh, groovy. Contemporary. I express bodies and feelings and how they relate to each other.'

'Christ!' I said under my breath. What kind of a nerd had I been saddled with! I stood up as if summoned by an unheard bell, said I had to go and like Cinderella made a bolt for it.

I didn't see or think of Val for another six weeks. Not till Fidelma came around one evening after work.

'Hey, Lynn,' she said, 'we're having a 60s night for the musical society on Saturday. Say you'll come.'

I groaned audibly. I was suffering.

'Val'll be there. Isn't he drop-dead-gorgeous and he really fancies you!'

'I can't,' I blustered. 'I'm off to the country to visit the folks.'

I could already see spring outside the train window, fields of winter corn flashing past, a dusting of catkins on the trees, my folks making a fuss of me. I didn't need man-hassle. How could I, after Martin ditched me almost at the altar and took off for Australia with a girl he had known a mere few months.

Fidelma refused to listen to me.

'You're cloistering yourself. All work and no play. You might as well be a bloody nun. You'd have more sport in a convent. Cop yourself on girl! Your folks will still be there next week.'

I yielded, painted butterflies on my big toes, put on a purple mini, a long string of green glass beads swinging down to my stomach and headed for the fundraiser.

When I spotted Val, I wondered was it him at all. He had a more highly evolved look about him than I remembered and seemed less overpowering, merging with the crowd, listening, rather than holding forth. To my surprise, I found myself hoping he would come in my direction, but when he did as if on cue, I didn't let on I saw him.

'Well, if it isn't the Banana Banshee herself!' he whispered.

The ice in my glass shivered slightly as my eyes swam into those greedy ones trying to possess me. That's when I knew he was still quintessentially him. He certainly looked different without the thirties gear.

'How's the art going?' he asked knowingly. I realised Fidelma had split on me, so I stretched out my sandaled feet. The glorious butterflies looked as if they were about to take off. I had studied their every movement in the Butterfly Centre in Carraroe. Watched them as pupae hanging from a twig in the over-heated glasshouse; sketched the first flutterings of wings, their flight, and now the captured stillness on my toenails. Stillness and patience were what it was about. If you work in miniature as I do, you must do your homework with precision as well as imagination.

'You're a manicurist?' Val was enquiring.

'A nail-artist,' I corrected. 'Flowers, butterflies, cartoon characters, whatever turns you on.'

I had no notion of elaborating.

'I think we've a lot in common,' he said smiling.

From that night in the Plaza onwards, Fidelma was forever begging me to give him a chance. It was on account of her and our friendship that I decided not to run him. There was no way I was bowled over.

*

Within two months Val and I had become an item. I never fell in love with anyone quicker. And that brought me back to the old chestnut, of speculating about love and puzzling whether it was possible for a man to love a woman without trying to possess her. Love is a discovery, one of the other. My experience had always been that the less you give away the better since familiarity invariably breeds contempt. That is why as a rule of thumb I keep an escape route at the ready, an emotional trapdoor that I can drop through at will. No man on earth was going to hurt me again. What I didn't realise was that by being evasive and trying to conceal myself, I was in fact revealing far too much to Val and that by moving quickly he had battened down my trapdoor before my very eyes. I might have been one of my painted butterflies. There was no escape. I tried not to panic.

Little and all as I gave away, I was conscious that Val gave less. He was ostensibly open, loving, frank, talkative. It was clear that he was very taken with my height. When he invited me for the first time to his workshop in Kilkenny, I was flattered, but not prepared for what lay ahead. Bear in mind that I thought I was visiting some class of art gallery, but this place smelled as antiseptic as a hospital. It was obvious from the inks, the needles, the general equipment, that my loved one was a tattooist. Sketches of the Sacred Heart and all kinds of religious images mingled with anchors and roses and snakes on the four walls. I could have murdered Fidelma. The bitch! Of course she knew. I felt such a fool.

'So, you express bodies and feelings and how they relate to each other,' I said with as much sarcasm as I could muster when I found my voice.

'Do you have a problem with that?' he said.

Of course, I didn't, but yet I did. I'd thought that Val might have wanted me as an artist's model; that I might have become famous like the wife of the French artist Pierre Bonnard who painted his wife languishing in the bath or draped against the garden vegetation.

I had met the real Val at last. Gone was the poseur and know-all. He explained how he listened to music as he worked; how he used the rhythm of the music, transferring it to his subjects. He demonstrated the amount of preparation that went into his pieces; how he realised his responsibility to his customers whose chosen designs were as much an expression of themselves as they were of him, the artist.

I think I was two months pregnant when I next visited the workshop. I looked squarely into the liquid eyes of the Sacred Heart, Padre Pio, St Christopher and a pantheon of unrecognisable saints. Did priests and nuns really wear the holy ones under their garments? There was Cú Chulainn too, and Mona Lisa, and St George and the Dragon. Val himself was wearing a yellow cutaway singlet which showed off to perfection a bunch of bright bananas on his left forearm and my name under them. His assistant had designed it under Val's direction. I began to laugh hysterically. He loved me. I thought how angry and defensive I had grown after the Martin experience. Now I had renewed confidence in the world. Val and I had a kind of ceremony.

'Does it hurt?' I whispered, looking at the needles and inks.

He tenderly swabbed my upper-arm close to the shoulder with disinfectant and deftly traced on it a single banana, his own name in the folds of a leaf. He worked gently, competently. I didn't feel a thing and the tattoo was very pretty, really much nicer than a ring.

Fidelma was gobsmacked when I showed her.

'Jesus, Lynn, you've tied yourself up good and proper! Why didn't you use one of those transfer tattoos? I never thought you had it in you. There was no need to go over the top.'

But there was. She didn't understand at all.

She continued, 'I can tell you I wouldn't do it... not for Val, nor any other man.'

'I'm not tied in any way,' I said proudly. I wasn't going to say anything further.

'Would you give over,' she laughed, 'Where else have you got a tattoo?'

Once we had a home together, Val developed a passion for gardening. Not on a big scale, you know, but in window boxes. The following spring, he had parrot tulips that would take the sight from your eyes. He was fascinated by their abandon and flamboyance. He looked at me longingly. Oh, I wasn't mistaken. It was my skin he coveted. Six feet of prime canvas. But it was mine. In the beginning, I was reluctant, but in the end, I gave in. I let him tattoo a yellow-red parrot tulip down my backbone. I lay on my belly, thinking of the child inside me and taking comfort and happiness from Val's hands drawing fine lines on my skin, the swirl of feathered petals swimming between my shoulders.

As for my own art, I shared it with him. Lovingly, meticulously I adorned his finger and toenails with wild flowers and insects of every kind. On the first anniversary of our meeting, I pierced the third nail of his left hand and hooked in a thin gold ring. Fidelma said that was different since it wasn't permanent.

By the time the baby was due for delivery, my body was a riot of colour. All of Val's personal feelings for me and our child were transferred to my skin. My gynaecologist's eyes widened somewhat when she examined my abdomen for the first time. Beneath her fingers, a serpent writhed under an apple tree and Adam was half hidden in Eve's tangled hair.

It was a wonderful picture. Eve's face resembled mine. Adam's face was Val's.

'Why did you do such a thing?' the doctor questioned.

'My husband,' I said, 'he's an artist.'

'Good God! And you allowed this? You do realise, Lynn, that tattoos like this are irreversible?' she murmured.

I understood. When I saw her worried face, it got me thinking once again of love and commitment and possession. Val was so obsessed with the living canvas of my body, would he ditch me when the canvas was full, or would he need me as his life's masterpiece? I got a chilly little feeling in the pit of my stomach when I faced the fact that our sharing was not quite equal. He could erase my nail-paintings with a ball of cotton wool soaked in polish remover. In his mind, love and the realisation of his artistic ambitions were one. I prefer to think that he loves me in his own way. However, I decided not to hand over any more canvas for the time being.

The baby was born. She is now three years old. Sometimes I see her father look at her longingly, greedily as if he can't get enough of her. I see her eyes swimming into his. I keep a sharp eye on them. These days he is teaching her to draw little yellow bananas.

Deirdre Brennan is a bilingual writer of poetry, short stories and drama. Born in Dublin, she spent most of her youth in Clonmel and Thurles and has lived in Carlow for many years. A founder member of Éigse Carlow Arts Festival in 1978, she is the recipient of many prizes including *Poetry Ireland* Choice of the Year (1989), *THE SHOp* poetry translation award (2002), Oireachtas awards for poetry and radio drama and a Listowel Writers Week short story award (1996). She has published twelve collections of poetry to date, the most recent being *Medea's Cauldron* (2022). Her short story collections include: *An Banana Bean Sí agus Scéalta Eile* (2009) and *Staying Thin for Daddy* (2016).

This story will appear in an anthology of translations of contemporary Irish-language short fiction (by a mix of translators), *Scheherazade's Irish Stepsisters: Contemporary Short Stories in Irish by Women Writers*, forthcoming from Parthian in late 2025.

WHOSE WALES?

The Battle for Welsh Devolution and Nationhood, 1880–2020

ALUN GIBBARD & GWYNORO JONES

> 'We're in the 21st century with an increasingly self-governing Wales. We were not meant to be here. This book shows how we survived.'
> **CARWYN JONES**

> 'provide[s] irrefutable evidence that people from all four political parties in Wales played a role in promoting the cause of home rule.'
> **MARTIN SHIPTON**

PARTHIAN   £14.99   www.parthianbooks.com   **Out February 2025**

ECOLOGICAL LITERACY

STEVEN LOVATT EXPLORES RECENT BOOKS THAT SEEK TO RESTORE NATURAL AND CULTURAL ECOLOGIES AND RECOGNISE HOW THE CULTURAL NATURE OF OUR LANDSCAPES IS PRESERVED IN LANGUAGE

From the top floor of our house in Swansea, in rare clear weather the view is right around the bay. To the south is Lundy and the Devon coast, to the west the dislocated crab claw of Mumbles. And if you look east beyond the steelworks, at the distal of your vision lies the great dune system of Cynffig, a slight thickening of the horizon between Port Talbot and Porthcawl.

These dunes did not always extend so far. When Anglo–Norman invaders arrived behind them in the mid twelfth century they were fewer, sewn to the shoreline by wildflower roots. The site was defensible, the prospects pleasant, and it seemed altogether a good place to throw up a castle against the dispossessed Cymry. Before long the population of Cynffig bulged beyond the walls and formed a dependent town. As was their custom, the Normans had brought rabbits, and on the dunes they established a burrows where the animals were kept for food and fur, alongside many cattle. The animals fed on the flowers, and over years the sand was loosened. The dunes that to the conquerors had seemed a stable part of the landscape proved anything but, and the volatile weathers of the Medieval Warm Period began to push them inland. By the fourteenth century the castle was engulfed and not long afterwards the town itself was abandoned.

The parable of Cynffig dramatises how ignorance of local landscapes and disregard of indigenous knowledge – those reliable blind-spots of colonialism – damage natural and cultural ecologies alike. This is the blight identified by Carwyn Graves in his new book *Tir: The Story of the Welsh*

Landscape (Calon, 2024), and his remedy is a return to the low-input sustainable agriculture – based on lived knowledge of the land and its capacities – that characterised rural Wales prior to the postwar technology and consumer boom, and all the artificial stimulants (financial and chemical) that accompanied it. Graves argues that such small-scale farming was the signature activity of a communitarian and ecologically literate society, celebrated by and fully partaking in a millennia-old tradition of Welsh-language lore that now holds a key to its restitution. These claims are developed and defended with clarity and passion, and *Tir* intervenes persuasively at a crucial moment when many Welsh ecosystems are at breaking point and the Welsh Sustainable Farming Scheme (SFS) is unconscionably snarled up in Senedd politics.

True to its subtitle, *Tir* grounds its arguments in seven central chapters, each of which examines a characteristic aspect of the Welsh landscape: Coed, Cloddiau, Cae, Ffridd, Mynydd, Rhos and Perllan. Each heading is glossed by a list, for none can be fixed with a satisfactory single-word equivalent in English. Rhos, for example, brackets 'Heath, moor and bog/wetter, rough grazing land'. Graves has a rhetorical as well as a factual reason for highlighting this asymmetry: in English, the terms before the stroke normally denote 'habitats', and are implicitly non-human and 'wild', while post-stroke, the reference is plainly to farming and a human landscape. By demonstrating that 'rhos' encompasses all these meanings, Graves strengthens a claim made in his Introduction about the significance of the Welsh cynefin making no distinction between the special haunts of animals and of people: 'the [Welsh] language itself naturally associates wild species' relationship to their ecological niche with domestic animals' home range and peoples' own deeply rooted sense of home.' Two further didactic points are promoted in Graves' patient explanations of these cynefinoedd: first, that Wales' landscapes, because they have for millennia been cultural, can and should be historicised for knowledge about how they were used and valued prior to industrialised agriculture; second, that the Welsh language is the unique repository of this knowledge.

For all the relentless spoiling tactics of agro-industrial lobbyists, sustainable farming practices are closer to mainstream discussions about land-use than they have been for two generations. On this level, *Tir* slips smoothly into what is by now an international conversation, and draws similar conclusions to many other commentaries about the disastrous wrong turn into fossil-fuel-driven food production and the need to recover more locally rooted forms of land stewardship. Yet *Tir* doesn't simply transfer general insights about sustainable farming into a Welsh context, but maintains that Wales is singularly well-equipped to recover a circular agricultural economy. In part this is because, although it has suffered terrible losses since the mid-twentieth century – 95% of orchards grubbed up, almost all hay meadows lost to intensive agriculture – Wales possesses just enough vestigial habitats and traditional land-management practices to re-seed a revival. Despite all that its landscapes and culture have borne, Graves argues that Wales finds itself in a more favourable position than either Ireland or Scotland, the first having lost almost all of its old forests, and the latter having suffered the forced dispossession of the Clearances, which all but broke the lived bond between land and people.

Though I referred just now to an ongoing 'conversation' about the future of Welsh land-use and farming, readers will know that this is too polite a term for what more often resembles a brawl. And while it should always be kept in mind whose interests are served by exaggerating divisions between Welsh farmers and rewilders – part of which involves caricaturing both groups as homogenous and obdurate blocs – there's no question that on some fundamentals the disagreements are real and intractable. At first sight Graves might be read as advocating a middle ground. Aware that 'the current agricultural economy is unsustainable at every level,' he nonetheless rebuts those advocates of rewilding the Welsh landscape who – in treating it as a tabula rasa – reprise the colonial mindset of the settlers of Cynffig or (more recently) the enthusiasts for Sitka plantations in mid Wales or English second-home owners. But it's quickly apparent that Graves isn't aiming for some bland imagined neutrality between the more utopian rewilders and advocates of the status quo. He sees them, in fact, as two sides of the same imperial coin and rejects both in favour of the home-grown solution, rooted in Welsh culture, that I have outlined. Along the way, Graves performs a great service to his English-language readership by explaining why the etymology of diwylliant (culture, based on the concept of 'unwilding') makes it likely that Welsh speakers will understand rewilding as 'unculturing'; his own proposal for the future of Welsh land-use takes a native culture of land husbandry as its starting point and develops it into an intelligent and generally well evidenced polemic.

Whatever its author might intend, the greatest value of a good polemic is often not to settle conflicts in its favour but by the increased scrutiny it generates to illuminate and test the validity of rival claims on every side, thereby highlighting the inadequacy of simplistic divisions between, say, Left and Right, famers and conservationists, progress and reaction. *Tir* is exemplary in this way. To mention just one case, the book should discomfort leftists who have not thought hard enough about the fine line between celebrating cultural particularity and condemning nativism. But there are also valid doubts about how well Graves' own arguments withstand the heightened exposure they apply to others. While Graves briefly acknowledges commonalities between the Welsh and other peoples who have been disenfranchised from their cultural traditions, and though he disavows an essentialist reading of Welsh farming culture, some readers may remain uncomfortable with what feels like the exceptionalism inherent in his approach.

For the most part, such reservations are inapposite. It would be mischief to argue against Graves' framing of the present crisis as caused by globalised, profit-driven industrialised farming, with the eradication of national and local traditions no mere collateral but essential to its logic. And in this context it's surely true that the sustainable land practices he wishes to recover will involve national, regional and local ways of knowing the land that are primarily in the gift of farmers, many having Cymraeg as their first language. Moreover – and elusive though it might sometimes be – in Wales there really is a palpable and culturally enshrined affinity between land and people, in which farmers naturally occupy a central role. Yes, this affinity is often terribly romanticised, and it can be difficult to distinguish the moist-eyed myth from the echoes of a real tradition that return slower each year. Graves himself is aware – whether fully or flickeringly is hard to say – that 'the story of the Welsh landscape' is bound up in idealisations, and he sometimes betrays these himself in how he describes people he approves of, as when one farmer is called 'a cultural stalwart from the valley'. But though they do need keeping an eye on, I don't think there's anything inherently objectionable about such effusions. The expectation that a well-evidenced argument should for that reason be devoid of passion is both illogical and contrary to a Welsh rhetorical tradition – if we stop short of calling it a disposition – that criticism should be able to accommodate without much suspicion.

The broader point is that sceptics shouldn't hurry to dismiss what remains an extremely important part of Welsh cultural distinctiveness, nor to discount its potential to be harnessed for either reactionary or progressive purposes – all the more so, in fact, if it has a strong self-mythologising element. In his excellent *Shaping the Wild: Wisdom from a Welsh Hill Farm* (strongly recommended as a companion to *Tir*), David Elias notes that for at least three generations Welsh farmers have been incentivised in the wrong direction and that this has given rise to a 'largely unconscious mindset of increased production'. Though he is under no illusion that it will be easy, Elias argues that this mindset needs to be understood and then gradually altered to a point where farmers are able to see food production as only one aspect of their work, and take equal pride in their role as ecological custodians. When the farmers *are* the conservationists, the present gulf of understanding between the two will have been bridged in the best way possible.

Elias is readier than Graves to admit that many, perhaps most, Welsh farmers are lukewarm at best about proposals for wildlife conservation and sustainability, but both authors are rightly adamant that the necessary changes to land-use will be impossible to achieve without them. And there is no prospect of bringing more farmers onside if the public money made available through the SFS does not exceed the sum of all the grants and subsidies they currently rely on; the latter is in any case inadequate when set against rising inflation and the costs involved, for example, in complying with new anti-pollution regulations and the slaughter of cattle in the battle against bovine TB. It is a fantasy to expect a change of mindset without ample and sustained financial support that is sensitive to local difference and informed by local knowledge.

For all the validity of Graves' emphasis on traditional Welsh farming cultures, though, *Tir* remains open to criticism that it is sometimes unnecessarily one-sided and exclusionary in what it downplays or omits. Graves seems to hold the Enlightenment responsible for distorting or destroying an essentially pre-modern contract between people and land, a contract written not in words but in work, and his own Romantic and Christian sympathies emerge in rhetoric that's pronouncedly wary of the modern and the urban. Granted, one could make a strong case that these sympathies are both a distinctive and valuable characteristic of the Welsh cultural makeup and a necessary counterweight to the secular rationalism that has laid waste to the world, but this is not why I find them problematic. Graves' biases matter here because they seemingly forbid him from acknowledging that his nostalgia for community and a vita activa in harmony with the natural world will be shared by a much wider and more diverse readership than he seems to be addressing. Though the book suggests no overt prejudice, it would be reasonable for suburban permaculture enthusiasts, say, or the refugees involved in planting community gardens in the cities of south Wales to question whether the valorisation of rural Welsh-speaking farmers need happen at their implied expense.

A defender of Graves' approach might counter that the constant effort to be fully inclusive, regardless of its sincerity or even its possibility, is liable to dilute necessary arguments about particularities into platitudes fit only for ammunition in the culture wars. Readers will make up their own minds, but this is another example of how a forceful polemic can show up tensions that are usually avoided because they are uncomfortable. I consider Graves' special and intense focus on Welsh farming cultures to be both well justified and well advertised. But though I recommend *Tir* to everyone who shares his concerns, there's no doubt that he sometimes paints himself into a corner. When he castigates the Welsh Government for 'borrow[ing] from global discourse rather than sensitively understand[ing] place and its dynamics', and concludes from this that 'governance in Wales remains, from a biophysical point of view, insufficiently Welsh', one may readily agree with him yet still feel that some global discourses might be more helpful than others. Graves himself, it will be remembered, upholds the value of traditional Welsh farming practices partly with reference to a recent 'indigenous turn' in the environmental humanities that is substantially derived from the work of feminist ethnographers. This suggests not only the folly and futility of any attempt to separate oneself from international conversations, but also to the existence of surprising alliances cutting across the stereotyped binaries of Welsh/conservative/patriarchal vs global/ecofeminist/Left.

It is easy to engage with *Tir*'s polemics, one way or the other, because they are presented so clearly, and it's to Graves' great credit that a book which could very easily have been dry and 'niche' is anything but. He has a calm, authoritative voice, and his assertions about the Welsh landscape, its uses and abuses, are helpfully supported by endnote references that respect the reader's judgement and prevent the arguments ever becoming shrill. The various argots of academia, environmental science and policymaking are subsumed into a readable vernacular, Graves adopting the currently fashionable style of nature writing in which the author's own knowledge is supplemented by encounters in the field – here, with a number of small-scale, traditionally practising farmers throughout Wales. This kind of voice is deceptively difficult to get right, but Graves steers successfully between grandiloquence and chumminess. And though he shows in places that he is a capable lyrical writer, he exerts wise restraint and keeps the focus on his argument. The body chapters all follow a similar pattern whereby a particular sort of cynefin is introduced and related to historical forms of maintenance and harvesting before Graves meets and learns from an embattled relict practitioner and concludes, convincingly, that profitable farms, healthy diets and richly biodiverse landscapes are all attainable if we would only rediscover the practical wisdom of our farming forebears. If his conservatism leads him to place greater stress on the recovery of old techniques than the part that modern technology can play in regenerative farming, then this is no fatal flaw.

Tir differs from other books concerned with sustainable land use, not only in its geographical focus on Wales but also because it makes so much of literary tradition. It's not uncommon for authors of environmental or 'nature' writing to decorate field reportage or popular science with literary extracts, but as we've seen, *Tir* has a different and deeper reason to engage with a Welsh poetic heritage that Graves interprets as having a custodial role in preserving forms of practical land stewardship. He asserts that 'the Welsh poetic tradition has been at the core of the culture's conception of itself, the land and nationhood', and he demonstrates this very ably – up to a point. Certainly, the quotations and literary interpretations included throughout *Tir*, from the likelihood that the Tale of Culhwch and Olwen contains a folk memory of Iron Age tree harvesting, to fine medieval and early modern poems showing love and intimate knowledge of worked Welsh landscapes, support what Graves has to say.

Here again though, a case strengthened by its inclusions is undermined by significant omissions. On the most basic level there are simply too few literary extracts for the reader to feel that Graves fully makes good on his ambitions for *Tir*. There are also imbalances in what he has selected for quotation: the majority of the extracts are several centuries old, such that a reader unfamiliar with contemporary Welsh literary culture would not guess that the tradition of environmental poetry in Cymraeg is very much alive. It is also unfortunate, I think, that the nature and scope of *Tir*'s argument oblige Graves to ignore the contribution of Welsh poetry in English, which has long shared many of the same concerns as its Cymraeg counterpart (not to mention the many Welsh poets who have written environmental poems in both languages). For example, it seems awkward, in the context of Graves' criticism of how former ffridd was destroyed by compulsory purchase for conifer plantations, to overlook Ruth Bidgood's fine poetry on just this theme. In her Foreword, Gillian Clarke twice states that *Tir* is equally reverent of both Welsh- and English-language culture and literature, but in truth the book doesn't support such an ecumenical reading.

Graves' keenness to claim for Welsh poetry a special concern with agriculture and with concrete, place- and time-specific imagery also leads him, at times (inevitably) into another form of the apparent exceptionalism that I have already noted. Of a poem by Iolo Goch, Graves rightly claims that by its specific references to farming it differs from pastoral idylls imported from continental Europe, but – whether wittingly or not – he declines to mention that the poem fits very well within a pan-European tradition of *georgic* poetry, and relies heavily on staple georgic tropes. I don't claim that Goch's use of these conventions weakens what is a very fine poem – it does not. But Grave's analysis of the poem is incomplete to the point of making him vulnerable to charges of special pleading.

Early in *Tir*, Carwyn Graves articulates a key tenet of anticolonial criticism to the effect that the local is not the parochial. *Everywhere* is 'local', and local places should not be valued in relation to some supposedly superior centre but rather for the unique interplay of their particulars – for the distinct forms of life they constitute and sustain. Rae Howells' new poetry collection, *This Common Uncommon* (Parthian, 2024) is a fierce and loving affirmation of the local, exemplifying the sort of care-full attention to the interdependence of people, other animals and plants that will be required if anything worthwhile is to be saved from the present ruin. It's a book about a small patch of common – 'just an old scrubby wasteland' as Howells calls it, tongue in cheek – which Graves would recognise as rhos, right on the edge of suburban Swansea.

Even more so than *Tir*, *This Common Uncommon* is a book with a purpose. The common of the title – called West Cross Common by Howells and the other people who live by it and value it for what it is – to Swansea City Council is known differently as 'Land North of Chestnut Avenue', and is partially earmarked for a housing development. Part of Howells' intention is to 'sway some people to the common's side' in an attempt to fight this designation, but she also hopes that the book will constitute 'a record, albeit imperfect, of some of the flora, fauna and fungi that we've observed [...] in case it is lost in the future.' The anticolonial intent of *This Common Uncommon* is therefore on point not only because West Cross Common is owned, wearyingly, by the Duke of Beaufort, but also because imperialist attitudes and disregard of the local are not the sole preserve of distant toffs but also take corporate and bureaucratic forms that thrive within Wales as elsewhere.

So, *This Common Uncommon* would have been worthwhile even if the poetry weren't up to much. But the poetry is rarely less than very good, and Howells confirms the evidence of her first collection, *The Language of Bees* (Parthian 2022), that she is a highly adept poet, possessing one of the most distinctive voices in contemporary Welsh writing in English. Her poetry is popular in the sense that she writes for everyone, and keeps always within a colloquial resister, and though it is often clever, it is never intellectual, nor is the cleverness at the expense of feeling.

Howells is – in another sense, also – a poet of voices. In her Introduction to *This Common Uncommon*, she states her wish to 'get[ ] inside' the 'people, creatures and plants' of the common, and – if her small-'p' political purpose, as we have seen, is to speak *for* the common – as a poet she declines to hector. Between and within each poem, Howells uses fine adjustments of focalisation and tone to alter her readers' distance from what is described, allowing us to assemble a composite picture of the common without any one perspective becoming overfamiliar. Thus she also speaks *about* the common in many of its infinite aspects, and further exercises her range in offering lively verbal portraits of certain of its species and human defenders. Howells can write, when she chooses, almost with oracular authority, but she is not above a pun either. In 'A warlord of ecology', she evokes the Gododdin, light-heartedly but with serious purpose, when she says of a friend of the common that he:

charged down bulldozers,
besieged meads, skirmished at meanders

Even beyond this, though, some of the most striking poems here speak *through* or even *as* the common, Howells ventriloquising the land with great skill, humour and compassion. In brief, while the accessibility of the poems is never compromised, they present an invigorating variety and subtlety of aspects. Though it applies itself by design to a particular purpose and a small 'field', this collection is not an example of the single-use poetry that nowadays seem so prevalent, having plenty enough about it to reward repeated rereadings.

The collection's success as nature poetry is underwritten by its fidelity to the natural world. Academic criticism sometimes struggles unduly with this fidelity, usually on the grounds that we cannot be faithful to something we can apprehend, or 'access', only partially – partial being used either in the sense of incomplete, or subjective, or both. But the only fidelity required is the ordinary sort that involves a commitment to the reality of the world as it is experienced by the poet-observer, and this has always been popularly appreciated: 'nature writing' would not otherwise exist. That human beings are part of nature, and that skilled, sensitive writers can communicate both factual and emotional truths about it, was unproblematically assumed by mainstream currents within Romanticism and affirmed not least in the poetry of John Clare (1793–1864). Howells acknowledges Clare's inspiration, and the poems of *This Common Uncommon* draw on his example as a champion of common land and its various people (human and otherwise), and as a smitten witness of the world's independent life.

Howells and Clare have similarities, also, as poets. Like Clare (and in the Romantic tradition more broadly), Howells uses imperative verb forms and repetition to suggest that poet and reader are companionably abroad 'in nature', co-present, co-attentive, co-witnessing:

close your eyes. listen. willow warblers and wrens,
('stand')

> *things you hardly see any more,*
> *not since you were a child, but now*
> *growing here, and there, and there,*
> ('Commonplace')

Howells shares with Clare a capacity for unaffected approaches to her subjects that could be misunderstood as naive or 'green' in the wrong way. Most obviously this is the case when she uses personification. She sails close to whimsy in certain lines, to the extent that on first reading I feared embarrassment for them, but – except in one or two poems – her sometime homeliness is no less consciously controlled than her other voices, and her exactness of observation, verbal precision and botanical knowledge (in particular) safeguard against sentimentality. And when on subsequent readings I trusted more to her poetic intelligence, I felt freer to enjoy the bolder, delightful imagery of her personifications, as when sneezewort

> *sways inside-out as though*
> *a wind exploded through her bloomers*
> ('Sneezewort')

This extract also reaffirms that, though plain-speaking is a virtue, one needn't at all be literal to be descriptive. I have said that *This Common Uncommon* is anchored in the evidence of the senses and the immediacy of encounter. Sometimes Howells records her experiences very straightforwardly, and when she writes of 'butter-yellow' gorse, or 'the blue flash of a jay's wing', she might even be criticised for field-guide language. But this would be to miss the point. A blue flash is usually all you really do see of a fleeing jay, while the comparison of the particular yellow of gorse flowers to butter is also true to experience. There is an interesting and – dare I say – important discussion to be had (thinking back also to the *georgic* conventions I mentioned in connection with Iolo Goch) about the status of conventional imagery in contemporary nature writing: 'butter-yellow gorse' seems to me not a cliché in the way that, say, 'desolate moorland' or 'venerable oak' are clichés, but closer to 'wine-dark sea'. Might the literary culture of an individualistic society, suspicious of conventional language, for that very reason be more susceptible to verbal exhaustion?

Where conventional language is unavailable though, as when she seeks to carry over a picture of an unfamiliar plant or animal, Howells readily intensifies her descriptions with carefully observed metaphors that enable us to participate in her vision and the delight it brings. So we have a dragonfly as a 'toothed copter' ('Golden-ringed dragonfly'), wrens' songs 'scoring the summer' ('The common song') and linnets that 'drift like seeds / drown in their own sound'. Each of these metaphors is used with precision. In the downward movement of their bouncing flight, for example, linnets really do seem to dip into the fading trace of their own contact calls. This is knowledge that can only be had by observation.

And more broadly too, this book is greatly concerned – just beneath its surface – with different forms of sight and knowledge. In the kinds of knowledge it privileges, it shows significant similarities to *Tir*. Both Howells and Graves assert the value of lived and grounded local knowledge against the forms of knowing encoded in abstractions and systemic calculations, and both are – as we have seen – fundamentally anticolonial, drawing on Romantic traditions suspicious of rationalism and Enlightenment. Howells' Enlightenment critique is ultimately more interesting than that of Graves, partly because it admits more contradictions. The poem 'Follow the suckers of this nonsensical map' celebrates the common's unsystematic and changeable desire paths, yet Howells and her friends are aware of the importance – in seeking to protect it – of measuring it, counting its species and generally monitoring it in rational fashion.

As a lyric poet, Howells is able to go further than Graves in stating that the land itself is a knowing thing. The common possesses 'amphibian awareness' and 'spider sense', partaking metonymically of its denizens' various forms of sentience yet also, Howells sometimes suggests, mysteriously exceeding the sum of its parts. Arguably, Enlightenment critique is inherent, too, in Howells' repeated personification of the common as female, with attendant connotations of intuition, vulnerability, wetness. This visioning of the common as woman is not arbitrary: in 'Spell of protection', Howells grounds it in the Cymraeg etymology of 'Clyne', the area of Swansea to which West Cross Common belongs:

we invoke your ancient name: Clun –
you are feminine, you are hip, you are thigh

Other poems offer more playful critiques of masculinist reason and the cultural binaries of machine/nature, and rationality/spontaneity. One of them imagines the common, delightfully, as a 'clockwork toad machine', and Howells wishes it to 'whirr into motion, let it whizz'. But it is a strange, organic machine:

Without water it seizes.
Rain is the crank, the croaky ratchet,
waking the unconscious tadpole
in every dark pool

The poem recalls early modern hypotheses about the 'spontaneous generation' of living things from inorganic matter that nineteenth-century scientists worked hard to discredit, but it reverses the abiogenetic order so that it is water, frogs et al that produce a 'machine'. This clockwork toad machine is also self-consciously a metaphor, and thereby pokes serious fun at a rationalist tradition that depreciates the referential power of metaphor yet consistently fails to recognise the metaphorical dependency of its own terms ('hardwired' traits, 'selfish' genes, etc). This poem also aligns in fascinating ways both with the contemporary revival of interest in animism and hylozoism within the humanities and surprising events in the natural sciences such as the recent discovery of oxygen-producing but apparently inorganic metal 'nodules' deep in the ocean.

This Common Uncommon carries over from *The Language of Bees* persistent imagery of a feminised Earth clad in vegetation. The common wears a 'ferny blouse' and she covers herself with 'cloth / of bracken and gorse'. The potential for the Earth to be *un*dressed, whether in a loving or aggressive way, is suggested across several poems. 'A living autopsy of Clyne common' lists various 'signs of violence' inflicted on the common, before concluding 'Someone wants to have their way with her'. Confronted by such imagery, it is again tempting to delve back into etymology (and its roots in metaphor) and remind ourselves that 'divestment' can mean both the stripping away of clothing and political disenfranchisement.

If West Cross Common is developed for housing, nobody can now claim ignorance of what was lost. So whether you buy or borrow *This Common Uncommon* – and the same goes for *Tir* – be sure to share them widely. For there are countless such sites across Wales, all under threat and all uniquely valuable, the little-known places no less than those sometimes noticed in the media. Such fragments of the ancient landscape rarely make it into poems, and indeed I don't know that anywhere as small and 'humble' as West Cross Common has ever before been celebrated in a collection of such ability. But who will say that they are less worthy of care than the national parks and SSSIs whose establishment, as Carwyn Graves remarks, has not staunched the rapid bleed of biodiversity from Wales?

Unlike Graves, Howells advances no prescription for how Wales' landscapes might be restored. But the two writers are similar in suggesting – albeit with different emphases – that this restoration must be one of people as well as places. Howells' poem 'Common assumptions' acknowledges loss and forgetting, but hints at possible rediscovery:

> *Commoners don't even use it for grazing,*
> *No pannage these days, no estover. Nothing, no inkling, no coin.*
> *Just those kids down there, looking for glow-worms,*
> *remembering their way back into the blackbird's song.*

Whatever happens, and whether your starting point is 'No farmers, no food' or 'No bees, no food', we're plainly in it together. And there is no time now for tribal indulgences. The flowers have grown back on the dunes of Cynffig, but the storms to come will be much fiercer than before.

Steven Lovatt teaches study skills at Swansea University. He is the editor of *An Open Door: New Travel Writing for a Precarious Century* (Parthian, 2022). Steven is grateful to Dr Pippa Marland for her comments on a draft of this article.

Books Discussed
Tir: The Story of the Welsh Landscape (Calon, 2024)
This Common Uncommon, Rae Howells (Parthian, 2024)
Shaping the Wild: Wisdom from a Welsh Hill Farm, David Elias (Calon, 2023)

FANTASTICAL DOUBLES AND SPLIT SELVES

JL GEORGE ON RESPONSES TO TRAUMA IN THREE RECENT NOVELS

> *The moment Fetter is born, Mother-of-Glory pins his shadow to the earth with a large brass nail and tears it from him. This is his first memory, the seed of many hours of therapy to come.*

So begins Vajra Chandrasekera's *The Saint of Bright Doors*, one of the most gloriously unpredictable and challenging novels of last year (and which was out this summer in paperback). Like many a great opener, this snippet holds the wider themes of the novel in microcosm – in this case, the connection between the fantastic and a violently traumatic fracturing of the self. The shadow is common literary and psychological shorthand for a hidden or repressed aspect of the self, and in Chandrasekera's novel, its severing is what gives the protagonist his preternatural abilities.

A similar connection runs through all three novels under discussion here. It isn't the thread I anticipated pulling out when I sat down to write this essay, having chosen to compare the books – *The Saint of Bright Doors*, Carly Holmes' *Crow Face, Doll Face* and Lloyd Markham's *Fox Bites* – based on their use of the magical child or chosen-one figure. The child's-eye view is one important theme, but what leapt out at me repeatedly in my reading was the traumatic splitting, or doubling, of the self. The Gothic double has a long history, often expressing anxieties of class and imperialism from the perspective of the dominant culture, but can also be employed to more nuanced, critical, and inclusive ends. It echoes folkloric figures such as doppelgangers and changelings, and lends itself readily to various forms of fantastika as a result.

Of the three novels, *Crow Face, Doll Face* (published by Honno in 2023) is the least obviously fantastic: supernatural events appear to occur, but we are never quite told if they are real, and the novel remains grounded in the quotidian personal stakes of a family drama. The titular Crow Face and Doll Face – sisters Leila and Kitty – are the youngest of four siblings, but not the protagonists. Rather, the breakup of their family is relayed from the point of view of their mother, Annie, while her two youngest daughters become the proxies through which she acts out her complicated feelings.

Society-wide sexism is certainly at play in the way Annie's life has unfolded and the frustrations she plays out via her children. As young lovers, she and her husband Peter shared dreams of travelling the world, but once married, Peter confesses that for him these were only 'castles in the air'. Finding herself pregnant by a husband who wants only to stay put in their hometown, Annie abandons her dreams with 'brisk and total' acceptance, resolving to become a devoted housewife and mother. She never considers travelling alone: her opportunities are radically circumscribed not just by her husband's wishes, but by the imaginative possibilities available to her. We're not told when exactly the novel is set, though some cues suggest the 1970s. In any case, Annie, stuck in small-town Britain, remains untouched by the second-wave feminist movement. Attitudes to mental health are brusquely denialist. At later points in the book, Annie develops depression but receives no treatment or help. It never occurs to her, however, to rail against social forces like sexism or the absence of mental health support. Instead, her frustrations play out at the microcosmic level of family psychodrama.

Annie feels her first pregnancy to be a 'tiny, quivering bomb' that threatens to 'explode all [her] careful plans', putting an end to both her dreams and the person they have allowed her to imagine being. The bomb metaphor makes visible the violence inherent in the expectations that accompany motherhood, and the self-erasure that they demand. But Annie's suffering is deferred: her first-born, Julian, is a 'bright-eyed delight', and – for a time – parenthood is stereotypically blissful. After the birth of her second child, Elsa, however, Annie suffers from what seems to be undiagnosed post-natal depression and physically cuts herself off from her daughter, refusing skin contact, for fear that her inability to love the baby will communicate itself physically. This is where the cracks in Annie and Peter's marriage begin to appear. When Annie confesses her feelings, Peter is not sympathetic but 'shocked at the very thought that a mother might not love her child instinctively', and their relationship becomes coloured by suspicion and resentment.

When Kitty – nicknamed Doll Face for her beauty – and raven-haired Leila, or Crow Face, are born, things become even more complicated. Annie finds herself growing jealous of the sisters' intense bond and begins to harbour suspicions of supernatural goings-on, finding the furniture in their room moved around in the night though she hasn't heard a sound. The unexplained events come to a head at a family picnic, where Kitty and Leila appear to perform an impossible magic trick.

We're never quite sure whether these supernatural events are real or imagined. Although the children act out in response to their parents' divorce and the rupture in their family life – with Julian leaving to live with Peter and his wealthy new partner, while Kitty and Leila grow ever closer, getting into feuds with their older siblings and into trouble at school – the focus remains on Annie and her perceptions. The children become the battlefield for her internal conflicts. We see the splits in her psyche between the wannabe adventurer and the dutiful wife, the loving mother and the one who abandons her eldest daughter in a roadside hedge maze in the middle of a house move. Her buried desire for a more adventurous life expresses itself through a conviction that Kitty and Leila are special, magical children, lending meaning and excitement to her humdrum reality.

As her marriage falls apart and her mental health deteriorates, Annie holds the latter two girls closer, moving with them to an isolated cottage – abandoning Elsa, who is eventually found and sent to live with Peter, along the way – and sinking into a depressive episode. The girls begin to seem sinister, and Annie believes it is they who have goaded her into leaving

Elsa behind. This section of the book captures the stultifying frustration of depression convincingly, with Annie struggling to leave her bed and having to be chivvied outside by her daughters to attend their school play. When she's forced to engage with the world again, her faith in the girls' specialness begins to falter. Although she reacts angrily when they claim it was she who chose to abandon Elsa, she does also begin to wonder if they are 'just two little girls... [n]othing crueller'.

The novel's ambivalent ending points to the enduring precarity of Annie's mental health. Kitty and Leila appear to perform their magic trick again, and Annie is newly convinced of their preternatural abilities, restating her determination to '[k]eep them safe, as only I knew how'. Given her recent behaviour, this resolution takes on a sinister cast.

Annie is often an unlikable protagonist, and the narrative could easily tip over into tired horror clichés about mental health – but for the most part, Holmes' careful and humane foregrounding of her perspective avoids this, making for a sharp and unsettling look at motherhood and domesticity, and the pieces of the self that women lose in trying to fit these constrained roles.

Things play out at a bigger, society-wide level in the other two novels under discussion here – although relationships between mothers and children remain a significant theme. In *The Saint of Bright Doors*, it is the protagonist's mother who cuts off Fetter's shadow and trains him as an assassin, his purpose in life to kill his cult leader father. She is referred to not by name but as Mother-of-Glory, a moniker which both conveys religious significance and reduces her to her relationships with men. Chandrasekera does this deliberately: Mother-of-Glory's identity has been subordinated to the story propagated by Fetter's powerful father, and she sees her son as her only chance at reclaiming what has been lost.

The early splitting apart of Fetter's self sets up a kind of Gothic return of the repressed. Without wishing to give away the delightful rug-pull of an ending, discarded things prove difficult to get rid of. This theme is dramatised on both the personal level and that of the polity. Fetter himself turns his back on his mother's revenge crusade and attempts to live a normal life: he moves to the city of Luriat, where his lack of a shadow is politely ignored; gets a nice, middle-class boyfriend; and joins a support group for 'unchosen ones'. At one point he even adopts a whole new identity, posing as a higher-caste student in order to investigate the titular Bright Doors, a phenomenon through which 'devils' – invisible to most of the population but not to Fetter – can enter the city. His ability to see the 'devils' results from what Mother-of-Glory did to him, and remains a source of tension. Even as he investigates the supernatural, he must pretend it is invisible.

The city itself practises a similar kind of denial. Fetter comments on the

> *deep Luriati unwillingness to acknowledge anything that would require overturning their world, whether in physics or politics. A crowd like this wouldn't acknowledge the fact of a hinterland pogrom or a prison camp either. To them, such things are the invisible laws and powers of the world, to be left unseen or at least not looked in the eye.*

Fetter's own ability to pass unremarked-upon among the citizenry forms part of a pattern of unseeing that reminds me of China Miéville's *The City & The City* (a richly imagined novel which has been read as allegorical of everything, from homelessness to the occupation of Palestine). Luriatis remain wilfully blind to that which they cannot explain and to the fissures within their own city, the potential for violence bubbling under its surface.

But neither Fetter nor Luriat can maintain their façade of normality. However hard Fetter tries to be ordinary, he can still see the 'devils' – actually people written out of history by his father's actions – and however hard Luriatis ignore their own dark underbelly, their city's descent into sectarian violence feels inevitable, while its shadows are not easily banished. Even Fetter's own biography, as he conceives it – the story of a child soldier turning his back on the violence for which he was raised – has its double, a hidden story about the epistemic violence of colonialism and erasure. Institutional power allows its wielders to rewrite reality, quite literally in the world of the novel. It determines who is a victim, a saviour, a monster; who gets to live on the bright surface and who is exiled to the dark. Imagining justice requires paying attention to the others and to the abjected doubles of power itself. Chandrasekera's narrative conveys this in every part of its structure without ever patronising the reader, making it a challenge and a delight to read. Its many accolades are keenly deserved.

Lloyd Markham's first full-length novel *Fox Bites*, set in early-2000s Zimbabwe, takes a similar tack, colliding social upheaval – as viewed through the sometimes-uncomprehending eyes of a young, neurodivergent boy – with smaller, more personal disruptions. The young protagonist, Taban, suffers bullying and isolation among his peers after his family splits apart: his aunt, uncle, and beloved cousin Caleb moving away to a farm which will later be seized during land reforms.

Caleb has until this point been Taban's protector among the other kids, but after the move, he rejects his misfit cousin in favour of performing 'cool' masculinity, deriding the imaginative games they've always played together as being 'for dorks' and throwing around ableist slurs so that he begins to sound like 'all the other bullies at school'. This, he insists, is a necessary part of growing up: 'you've got to talk like the big guys or you have a rough time.' Taban keenly feels his inability to mould his self-presentation into the same socially acceptable form. He suffers vicious physical bullying from his peers as well as harsh discipline from his teachers, who react to his unusual way of expressing emotions with angry incomprehension.

Their treatment of him angers Taban, and rather than redoubling his efforts to be normal, he takes refuge in the fantastic. He begins to encounter a strange, vulpine creature that no one else can see, and to have dreams where he is a psychic revolutionary, Solomon, in a world whose history bears more than a little resemblance to that of twentieth-century Zimbabwe. At first righteous – nicknamed 'the Hero of the Revolution' – Solomon becomes increasingly isolated as he gains power. His wife Vashti, unable to persuade him to return home after the war is won, asks, 'Is your own judgement the only thing that's real to you? If so it must be terribly lonely.' His growing paranoia begins to destroy those closest to him. It plays out as a heightened version of Taban's anger towards both his abusive peers and the loved ones who have failed to protect him, feeding his resentments.

It's not only violence that bleeds between worlds here. On returning to his own life, Taban finds images, which he calls his 'fox bites', branded into his skin – evidence of his supernatural abilities, but invisible to those around him. He also retains some of Solomon's psychic abilities, and plans to use them to take revenge on his tormentors. As social and political tensions in Taban's world intensify, so does the violence of Solomon's – and Taban's world is revealed to be on the verge of being consumed by supernatural forces. There is more than one set of doubles here: Taban and Solomon form one dyad, of course, but other characters also find analogues in Solomon's world, where small, personal betrayals are writ large on a national and even existential scale. These doubles seem to represent not only the threat of violence, but also a level of awareness. Taban, because of his other self and his connection to another world, is able to see the threat to his own, and is left to deal with it without help from the adults around him who, like Chandrasekera's Luriati, maintain their denial, 'putting on a performance of normality'.

Taban must resist the temptation to become part of a cycle of abuse, thereby becoming a conduit for the destruction of his world. Although the stakes of the book eventually become world-threatening in the expected way of science fiction and fantasy, the story never tips over into rote spectacle: it remains grounded in personal relationships, keeping the story emotionally compelling. Markham also resists neat resolution. At the end of the book, Taban still has his fox bites, and even as he and his mother fly away from his Zimbabwe, he hears the creature's voice warning, 'You can't be free of me. I am born from you and you from me.' Anger and resentment are not external forces to be neatly defeated here. Rather, they can only be managed if they are acknowledged, recognised as a part of the self.

We even learn that there is a generational, cyclical aspect to the events Taban has been through. Taban's mother, Ann, was a previous conduit for the fox, and has their own doubled or hidden side, their nonbinary identity having been subordinated to the gendered roles of wife and mother. When they leave the country with Taban at the denouement, they are finally able to express their true self. We see integration and healing while at the same time being reminded that this will likely all happen again – if not to Taban or Ann, then to someone else. The work of resisting violence is ongoing because our other selves are never truly gone.

The dark double here provides a cautionary tale – and also a way of depicting political events through the eyes of a child who is unable to affect or fully comprehend them, but must still live in the world they create. Though qualified and realistic, the novel's ending allows a note of hope which stands out all the more brightly for the darkness against which it is shown. Like the other two books discussed here, Markham's novel makes inventive use of a well-worn literary motif, using it to consider the workings of power from a perspective not often seen in fiction from Wales. It deserves to be read far more widely.

Books Discussed
Crow Face, Doll Face, Carly Holmes (Honno, 2023)
The Saint of Bright Doors, Vajra Chandrasekera (Solaris, 2023)
Fox Bites, Lloyd Markham (Parthian, 2024)

JL George's *The Word* was published by New Welsh Rarebyte in 2021. An early chapter won the New Welsh Writing Awards 2019 Aberystwyth University Prize for a Dystopian Novella, while the whole novel won the International Rubery Book Award in 2022.

NEW PRICES!
newwelshreview.com/subscribe

Print & digital (UK): £20
Digital only: £18
Worldwide (print & digital): £40

LIBRARIES
Complete digital archive available shortly!
Print & digital: via EBSCO
Digital only multi-user subscriptions: via Exact Editions

NEW PUBLICATION SCHEDULE
#136 (winter): 1 November 2024
#137 (spring): 1 March 2025
#138 (summer): 1 June 2025

Image by William McClure Brown, 'Iolo Polo c2007, 117x76cm, Courtesy of artist's estate

START YOUR NEW YEAR WITH A STAY AT THE UK'S FINEST RESIDENTIAL LIBRARY

Read, write, research and relax at Gladstone's Library In 2025, you are invited to discover…

- Three beautiful and quiet Reading Rooms
- More than 150,000 printed items on the shelves
- Extensive archives
- Twenty-six unique boutique bedrooms
- Wholesome home cooking in our Food for Thought restaurant
- The cosy Gladstone Room lounge with an honesty bar
- Bookable work and conferencing spaces
- An on-site chapel designed for quiet reflection
- A picturesque setting in a North Wales village

Gladstone's Library | enquiries@gladlib.org | 01244 532 350

www.gladstoneslibrary.org

When you come out for the bell aged eighty you have no choice but to employ a late style.

This is mine.

MEASURING THE DISTANCE DAI SMITH

COMING FEBRUARY '25 FROM

£10 • 978-1917140393

Call for Submissions

Writing Back Home: Displaced and Diaspora Voices

Ysgrifennu yn ôl Adref: Lleisiau Dadleoliedig a'r Diaspora

رسائل الى الوطن: اصوات مهاجرة

Edited by: A. Naji Bakhti, Emma Butler-Way, Gwen Davies, Jacqueline Yallop
Publisher: Parthian Books
Deadline for submissions: 15 January 2025

Writing Back Home is a tri-lingual anthology (English, Welsh, and Arabic) slated for publication in 2025, that explores the idea of the 'imaginary homeland' (Salman Rushdie, 1982) through a series of letters addressed by members of refugee, displaced, and diasporic communities to their homeland.

This Call for Submissions is for the second section of the anthology, which will feature letters from Wales addressed to a reimagined homeland in the Arab Mashriq.

We invite original submissions of no more than 2,500 words around the themes of exile, displacement, and homeland, which touch on ideas of Wales as an adopted homeland, and/or displacement and exile from the Arab Mashriq.

Submissions should consider, in particular, the notions of spatial, linguistic, and temporal distance, and how these three factors shape the way in which the homeland is (re)imagined and addressed.

We welcome submissions in English, Arabic, and Welsh. Each letter will be translated from the language of origin into the other two languages featured in this anthology.

Enquiries and submissions should be sent to **anb106@aber.ac.uk** in the first instance.

WATERSTONES
WELSH BOOK OF THE YEAR 2024

£10.99

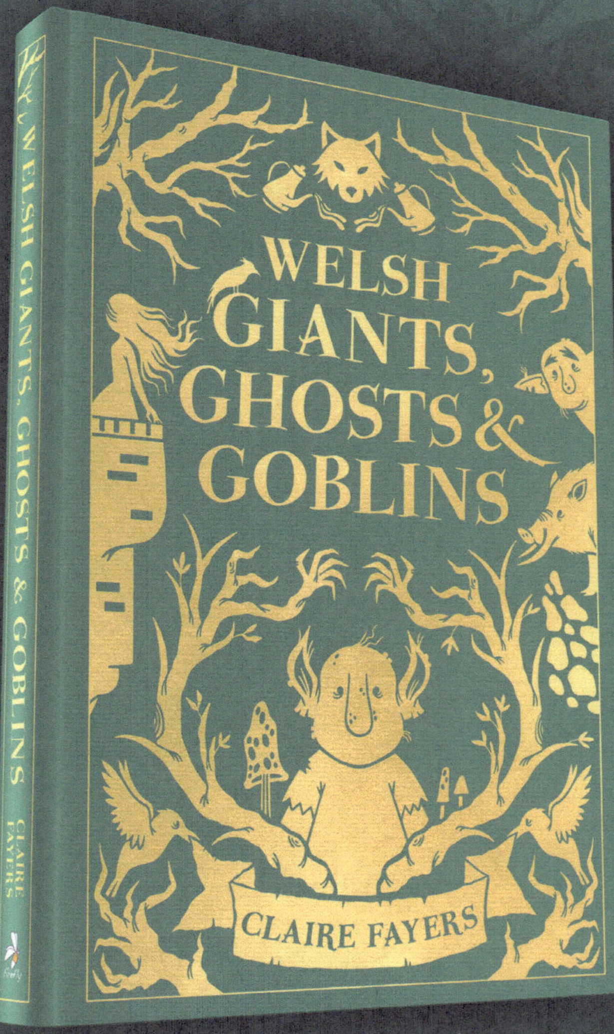

Welsh Giants, Ghosts & Goblins
CLAIRE FAYERS

HARDBACK EDITION
www.fireflypress.co.uk | @fireflypress

Association for Welsh Writing in English

35th Annual Conference
Gregynog Hall and Online
9–11 May 2025
Call for Papers:

Underscapes

What lies beneath? From drowned villages and underwater kingdoms, to peatbogs, coal-mines and the murky depths of the subconscious, we are troubled and intrigued by places we cannot see. Not yet defined by the *OED*, the term 'underscape' opens up perspectives from below.

Sometimes used in geological discourses of rocks and strata, 'underscape' can also refer to sociological realms of class, race and activism. How do the critical tools of our discipline get under the skin of a text? How do we uncover hidden worlds that have been blanketed by a canon? This call for papers invites responses to 'underscape' interpreted as widely as possible – from the figurative and imagined to the physical and actual.

Possible themes for consideration include (but are not limited to):
- Texts and textualities, close-reading and text-mining
- Geology and science
- Deep mapping
- Extraction, mining, energy studies, climate crisis
- Critical underscapes, neglected authors, works and approaches
- Psychology and hidden selves
- Relations between languages

The conference welcomes both critical and creative proposals, including work that reflects on the field or that demonstrates, in its own practice, ways of challenging or extending the study of Welsh Writing in English.

Proposals may be from individuals (limited to 20 minutes), from pre-formed panels of three papers (90 minutes total) or for a round-table discussion (90 minutes).

To learn more and submit a proposal visit: www.awwe.org
Deadline: Monday 20 January 2025